SOLES
defining
SOULS

LORI E. DIXON

Edited by: Deb Porter
Cover Design: Lisa Befus
Cover Images and Illustrations: Alisha Deddens

First Printing: 2015

Paperback ISBN: 978-0-9949395-0-0
EBook ISBN: 978-0-9949395-1-7

For Joy Hackett

A Penny Loafer who led her family with quiet grace and truth.
'Man will always let you down, but God never will.'

I miss you, Mom, but know that this separation is only
temporary. See ya later!

Acknowledgements

My deepest thanks to all the creative people who donated their talents, time and feet to make *Soles Defining Souls* possible . . . and fun. A huge hug to all of you, (except the Penny Loafers–because we know that you prefer not!)

My husband, Don who ploughed through my life, clearing a path to allow me time and settings to write. What a crazy blessing you are.

To my daughters, Tia and Mia who have put up with years of shoe talk. I know it got annoying. Thanks for letting me bounce off ideas and for being quick to say, 'No, Mom . . . do it this way!'

Nicole Dawson, and the *Christian Woman Magazine* community! Thank you Nicole, for giving me a place to be heard and a special thank you to the 150+ women who responded to my survey with such passion and transparency. I miss you all and look forward to sharing with you again soon.

Alisha Deddens for your awesome photography and illustration skills. Lisa Befus, for your countless hours crafting the cover (who knew that there could be so much debate over fonts?!)

To my daughters, nieces, sister-in-laws and friends who willingly gave their feet as models for the cover, and countless friends who met me over coffee while I rambled on about shoes.

To my editors, Don, Tia, Trish Keane, and the simply amazing, Deb Porter! You cleaned up all my mistakes and made me look good, (or at least tried). Your input and encouragement kept me at the keyboard. But I have to say . . . after all these drafts and months of edits . . . still not a fan of red ink!

FaithWriters–all of you–thanks for encouraging me to pick up the pen again after a long sabbatical. Your love, tips, and

critiques helped me to grow. Mike and Bea, you pour yourselves
out to see the Gospel spread. We love your vision and your heart.

A special thank you to the iDisciple family and Hal White.
So thankful I took the call that fateful Friday after Don's heart
attack when George asked, 'Do you have a book ready?' It was the
push that I needed.

Mountain Road Retreat, thanks for lovingly creating the
biggest, littlest prayer chapel! Your gorgeous, quiet setting was the
perfect place to craft the last four chapters. We are blessed to call
you all friends. Fire up the stove, we're coming again!

Contents

Introduction

In Soles Defining Souls, we'll explore various points-of-view of women wandering around the foyer and halls of our churches . . . and those who will no longer step foot inside.

Let's face it, the topic can be tricky to explore, but with a fun shoe analogy and some creativity, the journey needn't be excruciating! We can, in fact, take a painless peek into different sisters' soles to get some insight into why they "do what they do". Having taken that walk, we'll learn not only how to keep our own soles clean and in good repair . . . but also how we can stop stepping on each other's toes in the process.

My journey started a few years ago, when I was asked to speak at an evangelistic outreach for women of all ages. I was stumped trying to come up with an original topic. Rubbing my chin thoughtfully, a few fresh whiskies caught my attention, causing me to briefly consider chatting about the reality of midlife cruelties. (I could give the younger generation the good news/bad news. The good news is, as you age, the growth of your leg hair really slows down. The bad news is, that's because it's detoured, making its way up onto your face.) Running up the stairs to fetch my trusty tweezers, I plucked that idea right out of my head, choosing instead to spin my message around the unifying theme of shoes. It was a lot more fun to write and teach, and included the stories of Ruth, Jochebed, and the women of faith from Romans 16.

But something happened.

As I invited women to the outreach, I kept hearing the same message. They used to attend church, but left because they felt they didn't fit in, or had been emotionally wounded by others. They had no interest in going to hear me talk as they would be surrounded by church women. Thinking this was an anomaly, I spoke to a few Regional Directors from different denominations about what I had found. They concurred that the vast majority of church women are damaged and unhealed, and as a result, are hurting others. This cascading, daisy chain of pain has led many women to run from Christian fellowship. Those who stay are often hiding behind masks, not interacting and ministering to each other in the way the church was designed to function.

It was rather odd that in a relatively short period of time, I met so many women who had left regular Christian fellowship. I've learned from experience, when the Lord leads me into strange situations where I think, "What's going on?" it's because He is wanting to open my eyes and for me to take action. So I did.

I wrote an article for *Christian Woman Magazine* asking readers to respond to an online survey regarding their interactions with church ladies. The responses from over one-hundred and fifty women were heartbreaking, and confirmed this topic was both timely and necessary.

This international survey showed:

- A mere 22% of women felt accepted by church women:
  "In our church, unless you were born into the church, you are always a new person."

- Only 20% reported they can be themselves when around their congregation:
  "I'm a pastor's wife, and we deal with this as much as the women in our congregation!"

- Not surprisingly, 37% said cliques are the biggest issue:
  "The church I attend has a major clique, and if you are not part of that clique you are not truly accepted. I have attended for over fifty years and I am still an outsider. Very sad."

It appears that women have been dying to talk; to connect with someone—anyone—and share what they've gone through. For some of these women, I was that "someone" and I am humbled and privileged they felt safe to share their stories and their pain.

Please know my surveys were not conducted to *Barna Group's* rigid standards. I cannot verify the source or validity of every shared comment. However, I believe each woman's experience provides a glimpse into what is contributing to this trend of Christian women becoming unchurched or living less-than-authentic lives.

With the shoe topic still fresh in my mind, I found that the various responses could be grouped and represented by different shoe styles. Placing personalities on different soles gave a unique perspective. Now, for those who are easily offended, please know the scenarios and characteristics of the shoes presented in *Soles Defining Souls* are all in fun and in no way reflect any wearers of said shoes. Any resemblance to shoes worn or stashed in the back of your closet is purely coincidental. Please don't take it personally if your favorite style is slandered. Shoes do not have feelings—people do. Let's just get that out of the way.

Settling in to write the first chapter, I read through all the responses one more time to make sure I was conveying each woman's message correctly. Before long, I was in tears—again. The weight of pain experienced by these ladies was overwhelming, but their responses also brought out some old hurts from my past. Like many of these women, I was healed in some areas but still broken in others. Falling to my knees, I laid all of the burdens—theirs and mine—at the cross. I thank the Lord for each and every one of you who responded with such openness and honesty.

As time went on, I found myself becoming increasingly indebted to all who responded to the online surveys, who sent an email, or who called me. And to my dear new friend who made an international call to me, I cringe to think what that hour long chat cost you. However, we went from being strangers to friends and I am a better person for having "met" you. I look forward to a face to face latte one day!

So many of us are hurting. Or have been hurt. Or have caused hurt. Or all three. God heal us. God forgive us. I pray that this book, in some small way, may be part of someone's healing process. And if it only helps one woman, it is well worth my effort. Because every "one" matters.

Now before we put on our sturdy work boots, let's read some comments from a few of the survey respondents (lace up tight, ladies; some of these deliver a mean kick):

"I won't attend church there anymore; instead of walking away refreshed, I walked away wounded."
~28-year-old American Running Shoe

"I guess by the time you've been hurt and excluded so much, it makes it very hard to open up at all. I've learned to rely on Jesus and let Him be my all."
~39-year-old American Flip-Flop

"I recognize that I fall into the trap of putting my 'good Christian girl' face on while interacting with people at my Church. I struggle and sin just as much as anyone else but often find I have to be a 'good' example so [I] don't let too many people in."
~27-year-old Australian Stiletto

"As a person with a physical disability and a wheelchair user, I often feel ignored and of little value. Physical appearance seems to be the 'accepting' criteria."
~68-year-old New Zealand Mismatched

"These women are mean and ruthless all packaged up in the 'pretty, talented church ladies'. Gossip and slander is a way of life, and they can fool the best of them. My heart is grieved and crushed that people can act that way. I never knew that so called Christians were so vicious."
~50-year-old American Loafer

Ouch! But thankfully, we're not all bad:

"I think to sum it up is to say, 'they're lovely when you get to know them'. But it's not so easy to walk into an established group when you are shy, even if when you did, they'd probably welcome you with open arms."
~31-year-old UK Pump

And here's a different take:

"I actually have few problems with the women church members; it's usually the older males who should know better. In fact, if there was a women only church service, I'd attend!"
                                        ~47-year-old Australian Flip-Flop

Perhaps, once we get our shoes all straightened out, we may just want to try that once in a while.

Come take a stroll with me as we venture into The Lord's shoe closet for a brief, illuminating walk in our different sisters' shoes. Then we will examine the kind of shoe, or shoes, He's created each of us to be. After that, we'll hop up onto the Cobbler's workbench for a few needed repairs and adjustments.

Ready? Let's go!

Section I

Shoes! Shoes! Shoes!

Embracing The Whole Closet

But our bodies have many parts, and God has put each part just where he wants it. How strange a body would be if it had only one part! Yes, there are many parts, but only one body. The eye can never say to the hand, 'I don't need you.' The head can't say to the feet, 'I don't need you.'

In fact, some parts of the body that seem weakest and least important are actually the most necessary. And the parts we regard as less honorable are those we clothe with the greatest care. So we carefully protect those parts that should not be seen, while the more honorable parts do not require this special care. So God has put the body together such that extra honor and care are given to those parts that have less dignity. This makes for harmony among the members, so that all the members care for each other. If one part suffers, all the parts suffer with it, and if one part is honored, all the parts are glad.

All of you together are Christ's body, and each of you is a part of it.
(1 Corinthians 12:18-27 NLT)

1

Stella Stiletto

The higher the heel, the closer to heaven!

"Hey, Stella!" Much like the dramatic scene from *A Streetcar Named Desire*, our Stella Stiletto leaves an impression that is not easily forgotten. Unfortunately, the imprint is often left on poor, unsuspecting toes. She's a strong personality, and everybody knows and reveres her . . . or fears her.

Stella sat at the kitchen table with her Bible and devotional book open. Outside, the sun was just peeking out from behind the mountain. She sat quietly, taking in the sweet silence—the calm before the storm. Her husband and three preschoolers would soon awaken, and she would be thrown into overdrive.

Taking a few deep breaths, she lined up her colored markers on the crisp tablecloth while it was still clean, picked up her cell and snapped a picture of her quiet, still-life moment. In an hour the table top would be covered with sticky Cheerios, spilled milk and slopped coffee. Sighing, she uploaded the shot to her favorite app that posts scheduled, encouraging messages to various social media feeds throughout her day. A lifesaver! As the women's ministry leader, and a busy wife and mother, whatever she could find to make things more efficient was a bonus.

Having saved the entry, Stella clicked open her calendar app and let out a gasp. She had forgotten to order more of the church business cards, visitor records, and their popular little green *Jesus Knows Your Name* brochures.

What's wrong with you? People are depending on you . . . is it so hard to make a phone call?

Shaking off the inner condemnation, she set a reminder for first thing Monday morning. She wouldn't forget again.

Three hours later, Stella slid her manicured feet into her favorite six-inch spiked heels and clacked across the garage toward the freshly washed SUV. She was already exhausted, and the day had only begun. Just when they were ready to leave for church, their three-year-old twins had thrown temper tantrums, stripping off their tights and shoes, kicking and refusing to redress. Her husband Bob could not understand why she was fighting tears, as he found the whole scene to be rather entertaining. He captured the moment on his cell phone to share with his mom.

Soon, it wasn't just tears Stella was fighting. She lashed out at his insensitivity. His mother already thought Stella was an incompetent mother, did he really need to add fuel to her fire? With the mention of his mother, Bob's voice rose to meet Stella's and they began to bicker, both of them throwing sharp, verbal darts.

Becky, their impressionable five-year-old, had taken in the whole ugly spat and acted up too. Perhaps her mother-in-law was right. Maybe she was a horrible mother after all.

The ten-minute drive to church felt like an hour with the weight of Bob's hurtful words still hanging in the air. Pulling into the church parking lot, Stella's heart sunk at the sight of the bouncing woman waving madly. *Can't I have five minutes to gather my thoughts and pray before being needed?*

"Stella!" A serious, gregarious woman continued her dramatic dancing gestures.

As if she couldn't be seen jumping about in her oversized, unfashionable galoshes. Mercy no. Not this morning.

Waiting in front of the church was Betty Boot, the head of children's church, shut-ins' visitation, and maintenance ministry. The woman had her feet, and hands, in everything. Clearly she was going to ask for help of some sort. *Maybe if she wasn't spreading herself so thin, she wouldn't be bothering me every week.*

Plastering on a smile, Stella managed to speak under her breath through her toothy grin. "Bob, take the kids to the children's wing . . . and please don't share your newest shame video with anyone!"

It was show time.

Swinging open the car door, she flung her shiny shoes onto the uneven gravel parking lot. It was beyond her why the congregation hadn't raised money to pave it after more than ten years in this state. If the men on the church board had to navigate it in heels, it would have been finished toute suite. With determination, she pushed back her shoulders and walked confidently toward the wild, waving Betty. When Stella's ankle twisted beneath her, she went down on the ground like the post-makeover scene from *Miss Congeniality.* Jumping up, she competently recovered and continued her walk, smiling through the pain.

Having grown-up as a pastor's daughter, Stella had known her role well. She was bred to lead. To 'live up to a higher standard' as her dad would say. For a brief time as a newlywed, she had found a friend with whom she could unmask and be real, without judgment or condemnation. But, alas, a transfer had taken her friend miles away and they drifted apart. Stella had yet to find anyone else she could trust in that way. Women could be so catty.

Sure, Stella had over a thousand friends and followers on social media, but there was no one of substance in her *real* world. Being a ministry director, she felt the need to keep smiling and showing the joy and love of Jesus—regardless of how she really felt.

Oh, how she wished she had someone to talk to. Someone she could share her marriage problems with in confidence. She had once tried to talk to her mom, but as her parents' relationship was far from perfect, her mother's only response was, "You made your bed; lie in it."

And lie she did.

"Betty! Hi!" Stella enveloped Betty into a big hug. The warmth from her complicated friend's embrace felt good in comparison to Bob's coldness that morning. As much as Betty sometimes drove her crazy, she always made Stella feel loved. "How are you doing? You look a bit stressed; everything okay?"

"Stella, I hate to bother you, but since you asked, I just need to tell you that Pais . . . I mean, uuuummm, *one* of the women had to bow out of the Children's Church rotation due to scheduling changes at work." Betty shifted her weight from one foot to the other in a strange, nervous dance.

"Relax, Betty!" Stella said, giving her friend's arm a squeeze, "I've got it aaalllll under control. I've been meaning to speak to a few different ladies who don't seem to sign up to help with anything. God will provide the workers!" With a confident wink from Stella, the two entered the quiet sanctuary with only an hour to prepare before crowds would appear. "A joyful heart is good medicine, but a crushed spirit dries up the bones, Betty. Let's be sure to keep joyful. We don't want to be crushing anyone's spirit!"

❖ ❖ ❖

Oh, Stella. So many people are watching her. She's been stuck behind the mask of perfectionism for so long, she's struggling to breathe. How can anyone expect to be joyful and capable 24/7? As a leader, it's not easy for her to keep all the women in the congregation happy. In fact, it's impossible as she can't be responsible for anyone's happiness, but she learned as a young child that as long as she was wearing a smile, it seemed infectious to those around her.

And so smile she does.

This fictional interaction represents many of the Stella stories I've heard. Most Stellas are natural extroverts, but other times they are introverts, put into a sole that's foreign to their nature. Many have also been thrown into the bondage of perfectionism—often due to being the wife or daughter of a pastor, or part of an influential church family. As a result, they are often admired, disliked and/or feared.

Yet, a lot of women secretly wish they were just like Stella—or at least want to be her best friend. What they don't realize is that quite a few Stellas are desperately lonely for authentic relationships. They have learned the hard way to be very careful not to let their tarnished truths be known. Any gossip worthy tidbits would be fodder for the wolves. Public perception does not always equal their inner reality. No, they keep secrets tucked safely inside their soles and focus on the things they can actual control . . . like their meticulous reputations.

You see, Stellas are strong.

They lead with confidence and authority.

Our church ladies' groups need these powerhouses to help keep things in order, but in turn, we need to show grace to these "tall" soles! They are lonely, perched up on pedestals that most of them never put themselves on. Some may seem to relish the limelight and appear to be on a power trip, but underneath, many of these soles are hurting. Oh, how they would love to let their hair down, if only we'd accept them in their imperfection.

Don't believe me? Let's hear from a few Stella Stilettos:

> "I quickly realized that I wasn't going to be able to have a close relationship with these women, which is sad because I am also a pastor's wife in the church. I cringe at inviting them to my home or discussing anything more than the weather."
>
> ~43-year-old American

> "Being judged, criticized, and downright verbally beaten up for being confident. I am not confident in me. I am confident in who I am—in who Christ made me. I am confident that whatever God asks me to do I will be successful because He asked. I am often told I'm intimidating. I am an extrovert in a large group—especially if I am in charge—but an introvert at heart. I hate the phone. I suck at small talk. I am not comfortable in groups if I'm expected to just be a part. I am not warm and inviting. Entering a situation that I know is going to include a hug from someone I'm not close to makes me break out in a cold sweat. But because I'm in leadership, I'm expected to be warm and fuzzy. That confidence is supposed to extend into my core. And when the people around me find it doesn't . . . they're disappointed."
>
> ~No age or country given

"Can't keep up with the friends I already have. Why would I want to make more ... except that doesn't sound very Christ-like. I believe if I am confident in who Christ says I am then when offences come, the coat of His Radical Love for me won't let any hurts take root."

~50-year-old Canadian

"I have contributed to other people's pain through my use of words. I have strong opinions and sometimes don't hesitate to be honest. This can be good and bad. I have hurt others with an untimely word, a word lacking grace or encouragement. I guess arrogance or impatience would be the reason that it happened. Or that sometimes I want better for people than they want for themselves. I expect others to accept me for where I'm at, yet I'm not always good at accepting others for where they are currently at."

~No age or country given

"I love women and women's retreats ... I've had my share of hurts and my own 18-year-old daughter 'hates girls' ... 'girls and women are catty, mean, insecure and selfish'. I think it is a lack of obedience and walking in grace in their own lives. We need to expect less and be more filled and walk in the Holy Spirit."

~48-year-old American

"Gossip and slander have wounded us so bad, we left the very church we planted. It was 1,500 people and a group of wolves made it their aim to divide and promote hate. I've served as the leader of Children's Ministries, Women's Ministries, Church Office Manager, and I love people. This experience has me not wanting to meet any new friends."

~50-year-old American

"My biggest wound has been not having older women invest in me. When I was a teen the older girls didn't reach out to me and now that I am a young adult, older women in the church seem too preoccupied/uninterested/lack confidence to teach the younger women basic things about being a godly woman. They don't appear interested or willing to make the effort in starting a relationship."

~No age or country given

"Have definitely found cliques operating that exclude some people. Because I'm friendly by nature, I've had no trouble finding friends. However, I realize how hard it would be for a shy person or an unhealed person to find friends. Sadly, these are the ones who need it most! I often make jokes that I've survived 32 years of church life so I must be tough. It can be hard for people who are easily offended, those with rejection issues etc., because we are a motley crew really. Even I offend people without even trying! I've offended 2 women by accident that I know of, there could be more!"

~62-year-old Australian

Can I hear a collective, 'Ouch'?

These poor gals! It's tough to be asked to lead, even when it's your natural sole, but then to feel alienated and forced to hide behind a mask . . . that's a very lonely, uncomfortable place to be.

Having worn almost all the different shoes that we are going to be strolling in, the stiletto lifestyle is one I didn't think I had walked in. But as I prayed over this chapter—and these amazing, strong women—I realized there are times when I have worn and continue to wear these high-heels.

As a women's retreat speaker, I tend to slip into these uncomfortable soles during weekend functions. A Penny Loafer by preference, this is not an easy transition for me (from introverted flats to extroverted heels). The funny part is that I actually pack heels for my talks, which is a bit silly when you think about it. So why do I do it? Well, I do it primarily to dress the part, and to be "more professional" than the audience—something I was taught to do by the speakers' bureaus I've been associated with. Dressing up would give me credibility behind the podium. At least that was what I was told.

Good grief! I never saw how crazy and off base this way of thinking was until I wrote this chapter. Some of my favorite teachers have presented the Word dressed in flip-flops and t-shirts. What does it matter what I wear? I am a sinner, saved by grace. I stumble. My ankle has twisted beneath me more than once! I've hit the pavement and eaten asphalt. Thankfully, I've learned over the last few years to drop the mask on my first talk during opening prayer. I remind the women that God has spoken through donkeys (Balaam's donkey, Numbers 22), and that I am only a vessel—and a cracked pot at that—someone to be used by The Cobbler as He sees fit. I think this keeps things in proper perspective—much better than if I wore a two-piece suit and five-inch heels.

Wouldn't you agree?

But what about you? Are you a confident, extroverted leader? Or do you just pretend to be? Are you free to build authentic relationships? Or do you feel you can't be honest with the ladies you lead for fear they will lose respect for you? Or judge you? It's tough to be sure!

How are your toes, Stella? They've been stepped on so many times they must be tender for sure. We sole-sisters are so sorry for the pain we've inflicted on you, and for failing to accept you for who you truly are. After our little jaunt through our various shoes, we will all visit The Cobbler. He will gently release each of us from whatever is pinching or holding us captive. In the meantime . . .

You are amazing!

You are strong!

We love you and appreciate how you lead us and teach us!

But you're also human . . . and soft . . . and vulnerable.

Won't you forgive us for past hurts and give us a chance to connect with you? Won't you allow us to minister to you, just as you so willingly give of yourself to us?

How about we take a moment and poke around the sole of a Stella? Turn her around and around and see what she's made of?

A Stiletto makes a statement. She stands out in a crowd—often heads above everyone.

She tends to walk fast and with surety.

She's often colorful and splashy.

Her smile and laugh is infectious. She is quick to bring words of encouragement and confidence to those around her. If people are struggling with their life or ministry situations, they tend to run to her, somewhat certain that from her vantage point she can see a solution.

When a Stella walks into a room, she defaults into her leadership role and tends to be noticed immediately with her unique *clackety-clack-clack*. It's not to say that all Stilletos are natural chatters or strong leaders, but they have learned and prayed, dying to self and submitting to what the Lord has called them to.

Sadly, they often stand alone.

What I've learned from knowing Stellas, is that they can only feel free to drop their masks, be authentic and real, when they are surrounded by women who are trustworthy, authentic, and real themselves. Which we all can be after we spend some time with The Cobbler.

He has created and designed us for His will and purpose and as such, we need to embrace each other. Who knows—we may be called one day to walk a bit higher in a pair of heels ourselves. Which is okay, as stilettos aren't all necessarily tight or ill-fitting. I've been told some are quite comfortable.

Well then, what's the key to walking in "high places"? The key is to realize that heels only elevate us superficially. In God's eyes, we are all equal. No matter the heel, shape, color, age or size of shoe, when we become His children, we are joint-heirs. The Cobbler doesn't have any grandchildren. That being said, we are also all vulnerable and in need of healthy fellowship, true acceptance and love, regardless to our roles within the shoe closet.

So how do we help a Stella?

First of all, we need to pray for them. In fact, let's do so right now. Take a moment and bring a Stiletto before the Lord. Ask Him to touch and strengthen her, so that she would feel encouraged and refreshed. Ask the Lord to show us, and forgive us for the times we have misjudged, hurt, or held any misguided feelings towards a Stella.

We also need to allow Stilettos breathing space and show them grace. We need to avoid gossip, and shut it down when we hear it. A gossiper is like an old shoe—its tongue never stays in place. That's not okay. So not good. Let's just all agree to stop. Shall we?

Instead we need to exude Christian character that allows Stellas the peace of mind that comes from knowing they are accepted for who they are. They need to feel free to let down their hair, kick off their heels, and be real around us. When they know we are for them, not against them, they can lead in the freedom and grace of Christ—without fear of judgment, rejection, or gossip. And sometimes, we just need to say "I'm sorry" or perhaps ask them "How are *you* today?" or "Is there anything I can pray about?"

Can you even imagine our churches without Stilettos? We should all collectively cry out, "Hey Stella! Stelllllaaaaa! We love and accept you! Thanks for leading the way you do."

Betty Boot

Kindness is just love with its work boots on!

What would our fellowships be like without women who open their lives, feet, and calendars to an extra measure of ministry, work, and responsibilities? I'm not talking about those who sign up for one or two duties. I'm talking about the ladies we automatically think of when it's time to organize and staff an event, new program, or outreach.

Hello, Betty Boot!

Betty sat on the edge of her bed—her cold, bare feet dangling over the hardwood floor. She stared at broken, unattended toenails. How long had it been since there had been enough time for a pedicure? Rubbing her feet together, flakes of dry skin drifted to the dusty floorboards. You know it's time for a pedicure when you can exfoliate one foot with the other. Lately, every day was a struggle. The clock glowed 6:00 AM—time to give her mother her medicine.

Sliding on her slippers, Betty shuffled her way down the hall and quietly opened the door to her mother's room. Murky, yellow fluid trickled down a thick tube from beneath the sheet, depositing into a large medical bag lying next to the bed. Thankfully, the bag was not full, so she would only need to administer pain meds. The hospice nurse would come by before church to do the messy stuff, and would stay until Betty returned. Looking toward the ceiling, she closed her eyes and sent up a silent, *Thank you, God!*

This moment of thanks was one of many. It was only three years earlier, at the age of seventy-seven, that her mom had come to know Jesus. Prior to that, her mom had *known about* Jesus, but didn't actually *know him* personally. Sure, she had gone to church, been involved in all kinds of fellowship activities, and proudly called herself a Christian, but when she walked out the church doors, she never took Christ home with her. Church for her mom had been more of a social club than anything. So now, even though her mom's body was deteriorating quickly, Betty knew when her mom left this world it wouldn't be "goodbye" but rather, "See ya later, mom!" Betty left the room, another thankful tear forming in her eye, inaudibly mouthing, *Praise you, Lord!*

Two hours later, Mrs. Boot struggled to balance overloaded bins of children's ministry props and a half-dozen tote bags filled with print outs, scissors, glue and other craft essentials. Sheets of paper slipped from the bags and scattered behind her as she clumsily made her way toward the garage. She was anxious to put some miles between the house and herself. The knowledge that her mother was dying weighed heavily on her heart and mind. At least at church nobody knew about her home situation and she was free to be just "Betty". Not like at work, where she was, "Poor Betty", and the recipient of sympathetic looks and head tilts each day.

Betty thought about sharing with the church (she really could use some help with her mother, the house, or even a casserole), but as she was the meal ministry coordinator, it would just be awkward. No, she preferred not having to answer questions about her Mother; she just wanted to be treated normally for a few hours each week.

The decision to move Mom into their home, and all that entailed, had been an ordeal. Thankfully, Betty's husband had been very supportive throughout it all. But with his frequent business trips, Betty was the one carrying the daily responsibilities and the emotional burden.

Clicking the garage door open, Betty cringed at the sight of her filthy hatchback—yet another neglected thing in her life. Kicking off her slippers, she grabbed a sturdy pair of flat boots from the mudroom. They weren't pretty, but they were warm and cozy, and anyway, who would see them under her long dress? More importantly, they would hide her unsightly toes.

Cramming the last bit of supplies into the tiny car, she slipped behind the steering wheel, and buckled up.

She was off!

Turning into the church parking lot, the crunching sound of gravel brought comfort to her soul. Sanctuary and safety welcomed her. Betty felt more at home here than anywhere—especially lately. Pouring herself into church projects and programs gave her purpose and more recently, an escape.

When their last child flew the coop three years ago, Mrs. Boot suddenly found herself with an abundance of free time. That was the beginning of a rewarding season of ministry. She liked being the "go to" girl. It made her feel needed. Although, sometimes, it seemed like her ministries were the only reason anyone talked to her—when they needed something . . . or were bowing out from their commitments.

Yes, these days, when she heard her name called in the foyer, Betty often felt herself cringe. Was it a new request? Or an exit announcement? She could handle either, as long as it didn't affect her children's ministry, something she fiercely protected. That was her true calling. The other programs were okay, and she managed them because . . . well, because nobody else would and someone had to do it. It wasn't as if she minded—too much—but she did feel overwhelmed lately.

Still sitting in her car, a smile crossed her face when she shifted her thoughts to the morning about to unfold. Oh how she loves her time with the little ones. Last week when the preschoolers were encouraged to say something to God and the helpers would write out their words, little Becky Stiletto's note was,

'Dear God, I bet it's very hard for you to love everybody in the whole world. There are only five people in our family and we can never do it.' Kids are the best. They're so honest and forthcoming. Becky's truthful confession opened up a door for Betty to pray with her and discuss some heavy stuff on the little tyke's heart. She loved seeing Becky's face light up as she learned from God's Word and embraced Christ's love and grace.

Grace.

Oh, how I need an extra measure these days. I sure lost it on Paisley when she called to ask me to remove her from the Children's church roster. I really shouldn't have let loose on her. But to use her job as an excuse? So, she has a job. Boo-hoo. Most of us do! Except Stella—she is blessed to be a stay-at-home mom, with an attentive, hands on husband. No wonder she always looks so refined. Still, her home and life may look picture perfect, but last week's revelation from Becky spoke volumes. Betty couldn't remember Stella ever losing it. Her life appeared seamless. *Unlike my life, which is obviously unraveling and worn out. Oh dear Jesus, I'm not too sure what's going on in the Stiletto house, but please show me how to approach Stella and offer her encouragement.*

Getting out of the car, Betty slung three bags over each shoulder and stomped toward the back door of the church. She'd had a key for years and was often the first one to arrive on a Sunday morning. Dropping the bags onto the worn basement carpet, Betty quickly keyed in the security password to disengage the alarm system. A few more trips to the hatchback to cart stuff in, and within minutes, Betty had efficiently distributed packets and bags to each classroom. Once everything was in order, she moved her car to a proper parking spot, and then stood outside, waiting for Stella.

As much as she loved to keep her feet busy in service to the Lord, Betty sometimes struggled to find workers to assist her. There had been many occasions when she had approached women to help, only to have them say no. But when Stella asked the same gals, they were all in. *Go figure. Some people just have the gift of persuasion, I guess.*

Standing patiently in the coolness of the morning, Betty rehearsed what she would say to Stella. Too many times she had said things incorrectly and painted other women in a bad light. She didn't mean to throw sisters under the bus, but because she was usually rushed, she often ended up blurting things haphazardly.

All I have to say is, 'One of the ladies had to bow out'. Just say one. Don't drop Paisley's name; just say one. Lord, please put your arm around my shoulder, and your hand over my mouth.

She rehearsed a few more times, but before she could settle the butterflies in her belly, a bright light reflected into her eyes. It was the sun bouncing off the chrome on Stella's squeaky-clean SUV. *How does she always keep that vehicle so darn clean?*

Soon, Betty would be able to pass the buck to capable Stella, who would fill the hole in the Children Ministry's schedule. Oh, how she looked forward to seeing Stella and receiving one of her encouraging hugs. It always gave her such a boost. In the busyness of the morning, and filled with nervous anticipation, Betty became suddenly aware of how full her bladder was. When had she last taken a restroom break? Did she even go this morning before she left home? She couldn't remember, and started jiggling and dancing lightly up and down in her boots as she waved for Stella to hurry.

Only a few more weeks till Mom's suffering will end and she'll be with the Lord. Then I can take a break and deal with my out-of-control life.

Just hold on for one more day . . .

Oh, beautiful Betty.

She is loved and appreciated just as much—if not more — as she is needed. If only she had found time to let a few church ladies into her real world. Of course, if they had known about her situation, many women would have rallied around her and her mother! After all the meals Betty had coordinated, and runny noses she had wiped, she had major support waiting to help. So many sisters who would love to return the gift of service.

But she doesn't ask.

Because *she's* the one who joyfully takes on any task.

You see, Boots rarely sit on a shelf or are put on display. They're typically on the go, being utilized for work or to keep out the weather. Often, in order to protect their soles and prolong their life, a substance is sprayed over them to create a barrier, preventing

32

anything from seeping in or sticking. Yes, a hard surface is necessary to keep this footwear fully functional . . . but this can lead others to think that Boots don't care. Oh, but they do! Bettys are just often too busy serving to let their emotions show. After all, Boots are designed to be sturdy and dependable—not soft and mushy.

Yet, everything Betty does is done in love—for others and for her Lord.

Let's hear from a few of these faithful, often worn out soles:

"Sometimes I can be too honest about what I feel and say and have worked hard over the years, with God's help, to be tactful and consider my words carefully, but sometimes old habits die hard. I wouldn't ever try to do this on purpose but it just seems to happen. I find myself apologizing and asking for forgiveness when this occurs. I pray constantly for God's help in this area and have seen him move amazingly in me—which I find very encouraging."

~No age or country given

"Everybody is so busy, including me. I have had a tough few years but had only one invitation to dinner/coffee etc. over the last year. I have a strong relationship with God that has allowed me to be proactive and form relationships while others simply feel ignored."

~54-year-old New Zealander

"I have been very careful around the church women. We have been going to a large church for six or seven years. We have not been accepted with the 'right' people. So we were never invited to any events at church. Then we found a calling with the children. My husband and I have been teaching children Sunday school for almost three years. We have noticed the children will show you if their parents are good people, or are there for 'appearances'."

~41-year-old American

"Well to be really blunt, I find that many women of the church are not necessarily encouraged to be wonderful examples of lovingness and openness. Encourage them to be different than the other women they see around them in the world and then

33

you will begin to see a difference. Often they are exclusive and cliquey, rarely inviting in strangers or talking to them. And I find within a church community that has been present for many years that gossip spreads like wildfire and can break apart relationships. Please, don't complain about what others are not doing, but seek ways to HELP them however you can! This doesn't go for all, obviously, but I feel those are the major issues needing to be addressed."

~21-year-old Canadian

"I am a behind the scenes person, first to admit that I am not a people person, but have really worked hard to change who I am on a Sunday and when interacting with people, but because of my dual roles Admin/Pastor I have to be both. My senior pastor constantly tells me, 'Sundays you are a Pastor' but always defaults to me to do administrative stuff on a Sunday. For example, 'Have someone take that baby out,' 'Why is that not being done,' etc. I have been "told off" on a Sunday in front of people for something not being done. But I always cover for them because that's what you're supposed to do. I love admin but know that I do have more to offer. WHY CAN'T THEY SEE ME!!! And not the job that I do. I love my church and my Pastors but end up going home most Sundays exhausted and frazzled, and I know that I am not alone. I have tried talking to them, and they apologize but it's the same old, same old."

~No age or country given

"My husband is a Pastor and I have seen a lot of this. There are a lot of contributing factors, I believe, to this issue. One of which is the fact women are often times working and very busy. We are so busy that all we have time to focus on is our list, our agenda and our issues. We are so narrow–sighted that we don't think about others."

~32-year-old American

"Someday I'd love to feel that people like me for me, not for what I can do for them. It would be nice to attend a friend's baby shower or wedding or church event without being asked to be the person to coordinate it. ☺ Probably my fault since I've offered to do these things to make me feel 'valuable'."

~48-year-old American

"I am fairly involved in my church and know that, without meaning to, through busyness [I] can neglect to slow down and take time for people. I also know the lengths taken by my church to include people and make sure that they are supported [in] forming one-to-one friendships, not just the official 'here's a bunch of flowers from the church'. Perhaps you could write on the evils of busyness and the resulting lack of time for others."

~48-year-old New Zealander

Are you a Betty? Do you know and love a Betty?

Let's poke around a bit and check out these beautiful, hard-working soles.

They are the heaviest of the shoes due to the weight of all the jobs they feel called to do, but their loud, rhythmic clomping brings us comfort, knowing that gifted, giving feet are busy in joyful service.

Bettys are resourceful, hardworking gals. They truly are! But no matter how amazing they are at multi-tasking, delegating, and keeping several balls up in the air, there comes a time—a season—when they need to drop a few things. Knowing this to be true, they can't risk being compromised, so Boots often include steel toes to protect them from falling objects, destructive words and a misplaced sister's foot.

But don't be deceived . . . no Boot is indestructible.

Many Bettys can be at risk for not only surface, but penetrating damage. We other soles must not forget that.

And Boots can, and do, wear out.

Yet, precious Bettys rarely reach out for help on *personal* matters.

While most Boots have a lot of friends and followers on social media, they don't open up and reach out too readily. A few have told me that's because it's just easier to do things themselves. Others say they are tired of asking for help with ministries and getting shot down. As a result, when Bettys are personally struggling, they are often hesitant to ask for assistance for fear of being disappointed once again.

And, as for the helpful ladies who do jump in to assist at church, Bettys consider them a much-needed and beloved treasure.

Boots believe that asking those special friends for *personal* help would simply be . . . too much to ask.

These tired, lonely soles.

Bettys' homes are rarely picture-perfect. In fact, they're usually cluttered. They live by their favorite motto, 'Boring women live in clean houses,' (which some fascinating women in clean homes may successfully debate). Craft bins and sewing machines sit on formal dining room tables that haven't seen a tablecloth, proper china, or a guest in years. When a Betty is called on to host a meeting, or when she has people in her home for social reasons, she is most likely to provide simple casseroles, served on plain dishes, balanced on laps in the living room. Which is just that—a well-lived in place. No plastic on these couches . . . but oh-so-beautifully lived in!

On much the same note, their vehicles are not chosen with style or prestige in mind, but rather to facilitate moving props and supplies, and they always seems to be in need of a wash and vacuum.

If you ask a Betty Boot how she is doing, she will typically give you the latest update on her most recent ministry, or a testimony of praise for provisions. So you need to hear her, encourage her, and then take it a step further.

Ask Betty how *Betty* is.

You may have to wait or dig a bit. Remember, she's got those sturdy, protective soles and toes going on, so it takes a little longer than most gals to get down into her soul. But eventually, when she feels that you really do care and there is trust, she will untie those double-knotted, frayed boot-strings and loosen up.

Then we need to listen—and I mean *really* listen because this is the girl who is there for us, and for our children. This is the woman who graciously and lovingly attends to both sick shut-ins and dirty toilets alike. What a privilege to be able to help attend to *her* needs.

Betty is not going to lay out a plan of help for herself the way she would for another church lady. No, you're going to have to hear her needs, pray for discernment, and then go into action on your own or with others. She will say she's fine. She will say she has no needs. But if you hear her heart, you will find the truth.

If, while reading this, a specific work boot wonder-woman comes to mind, can I encourage you to write her a little note of thanks? Maybe include an invitation for a special cup of coffee, or an offer to assist her on a day project, or perhaps a gift card for a much-needed pedicure and pampering? (For our stretched-thin Bettys, a twenty minute pedicure can be as rejuvenating as a week in the Bahamas.) How about asking her if you can borrow her car for an errand, then take it out for an oil change, and a good wash and clean instead.

Of course, one of the most important things we can do for our Bettys is to pray, and to *tell them* that we are praying for them, their various ministries, and their families. Let's do so for any Bettys in our life right now. Take a moment and thank the Lord for these ladies. Ask Him to give them an extra measure of His Grace and to open our eyes to their needs.

We also need to make ourselves available to our Boots.

When a person is standing with an armful of responsibilities, it's not super helpful if we surround them with cheers and applause. We need to lift part of their load when we can, too.

Hello, Betty. Are these words making their way into your sturdy, tired soles?

How are you, dear?

Are you struggling in that heavy pair of dusty and worn work boots? I hope you don't believe you need to earn your way to heaven by good works. Good works are evidence that we are born again, and a child of God, but are not a golden ticket to enter into eternity with Him. No, we are going to learn when we meet with The Cobbler that there is nothing we soles can do to make eternal life in Heaven possible outside of true repentance and accepting His precious gift.

Betty, do you long for an easier season? Is it time for you to step out and pass those precious, bad-boy-boots on to someone else for a week, a month, or longer?

You should know, my faithful friend that shoes are designed for specific purposes and seasons; we are not "stuck" in any one pair. We can prayerfully kick off any footwear that no longer fit, even if only for a short period of rest. In fact, shoe experts tell us that soles need a rest and shouldn't be worn every day because they tend to lose their shape . . . or become stinky.

We don't want that now, do we?

So, it's okay to undo those double knots, loosen tired tongues, and release yourself.

And as for us, your sole sisters? We just walked a mile in your shoes and we've felt your struggles. We need to accept you and to lift you up . . . without judgment. We need to be there to support you so that you can just be you, and have time to flourish in the gifts that God has given you.

Betty, please know we love and appreciate you, and all you do. You are not unnoticed. Take a rest and don a pair of flip-flops for a while. You may find them freeing for a short, summer season. Or perhaps a soft-soled, penny loafer would be a welcome change for your tired tootsies!

Penny Loafer

*Finding love is like finding shoes . . . People
look for good looking, smart ones . . . But
somehow they end up with ones they feel
comfortable with.*

Meet our next sole, Penny Loafer. Everyone knows her. Well, actually, very few know her, but it seems everyone talks about her. She's been attending the church for over five years now and refuses to volunteer for anything . . . or so it seems.

Pulling into the parking lot, Penny was relieved to hear the sound of praise and worship music. Everyone would be in the sanctuary, allowing her to sneak in the back, unnoticed. More often than not, she arrived five minutes late every week. She was thankful her husband, Sam, went early for the elders' meetings—it gave her an excuse to take her own car.

Yawning, Penny fumbled through the clutter in the console, trying to find her reading glasses. Months ago, she volunteered to clean the local soup kitchen on Saturday nights. At the time, she didn't realize it would result in her getting home after midnight. Not that she minded. She loved helping out, and the serenity of the quiet kitchen soothed her. Working alone, scrubbing down the greasy stove and grimy countertops was, for Penny, an act of worship. Everything she touched, every plate she stacked, she asked Jesus to bless those who contributed to the mess left behind. With her prayer list on the counter, Penny conversed with the Lord, interceding for many as she cleaned.

Prayer is her thing. She loves to hang out with God all day long, and feels privileged to share and bear others' burdens, no matter the time of day or where she may be.

Having found her specs, Penny pushed them up on her crown like a headband and stared at the enormous church she called home. She grabbed her Bible bag, and then paused yet again. Her heart was grieved. No matter how hard she tried, no one here seemed to accept or understand her. Unlike Sam, who everyone loved. Penny's husband was a born leader, ministering on the church board and discipling young men. Naturally outgoing, he enjoyed greeting the congregation and passing out bulletins. Opposites attract, all right. For Penny, church life was not so easy, and being the wife of a popular elder placed a lot of unmet expectations on her. Even so, her depth and quietness complemented her husband's extroverted personality. Together, they were a great fit.

Sadly, many women in the church thought otherwise, and she knew what they said behind her back—that she was a woman who did not get involved, was not sociable, and did not deserve her wonderful husband. But they were all wrong. It's not that she disliked other believers or thought she was better than them. She loved them! But while her hubby showed his Christian love with a smile and a handshake, Penny demonstrated it privately on her knees.

Not long after joining the fellowship, Penny was excited to hear they had a prayer team. However, after attending a few of the prayer meetings, she became discouraged and full of anxiety. Shouldn't prayer teams sit together and just pray? As someone who struggled in groups or noisy settings, the idle chit-chat and tea before prayer made her very uncomfortable. Her husband was the one who suggested she arrive fashionably late and just jump in once prayer was underway.

At first, that worked well . . . until she was politely informed that her late arrival was inconsiderate, and she should come on time for tea or stay away. So as to not upset the others, she stopped attending. She didn't stop praying; she just did it alone. Since then, hardly any of the women spoke to her.

No matter, this was their place of worship and she was making it work. Unhitching her seatbelt and opening the car door, Mrs. Loafer could hear the volume of worship rising. She shuffled across the rough gravel parking lot toward the front entrance. Each sharp stone could be felt beneath her soft soles, causing her to walk that much slower.

Then she saw them, Stella Stiletto and Betty Boot, watching her from behind the big glass doors with serious, determined faces. *Trouble.*

"Penny!" Enveloped in a death grip hug, Penny struggled to breathe between Stella's ample breasts. The woman was an amazon in her six-inch heels. Pulling her head to one side, her eyes begged Betty to rescue her. Instead, Betty broke her stare, gazing down at her sturdy work boots.

Finally released, Stella continued. "Penny, we've been talking," she motioned toward Betty, who was busy trying to rub out a smudge on her boot. "We decided it's time for you to get more involved here. We need to encourage and allow more women to get busy, and we're starting with you. We've signed you up for children's ministry starting next week. Isn't that exciting?" Without waiting for Penny to respond, Stella smiled and continued, "The schedule is on the door downstairs. And remember, whatever we do, we work at it with all our hearts, as working for the Lord, not for human masters."

Flipping her hair over her shoulder, Stella gave Penny another awkward, stiff hug, then grabbed Betty's hand and pulled her toward the heavy, dark sanctuary doors.

Alone, Penny stood for a moment, trying to process what had just happened. Her mind raced to recall part of the familiar Colossians chapter that Stella had quoted. She had prayed it many times by heart:

'Therefore, as God's chosen people, holy and dearly loved, clothe yourselves with compassion, kindness, humility, gentleness and patience. Bear with each other and forgive one another if any of you has a grievance against someone. Forgive as the Lord forgave you. And over all these virtues put on love, which binds them all together in perfect unity. Let the peace of Christ rule in your hearts, since as members of one body you were called to peace. And be thankful."

(Colossians 3:12-15)

Not wanting to upset the church or her husband, she knew what she had to do. First thing tomorrow, she would call her doctor and get a prescription for the anti-anxiety medicine she took after being forced into children's ministries at their old fellowship. She loved children, and prayed over the Sunday school register every week, but it wasn't her spiritual gift to teach.

Wiping a tear, Penny decided to tidy the visitors' desk before joining Sam in worship. Opening the drawer behind the counter, Penny restocked some cards and bulletins. Taking a stack of green outreach brochures, she laid hands on the pile and prayed that they would reach those who were searching. *Lord, bless each and every hand that both gives and receives these!*

Feeling better having prayed, Penny pushed back her shoulders and made her way into the sanctuary.

Poor Penny. Months later she wound up in the hospital, suffering from chronic depression and panic attacks.

Now, before you jump on ol' Stella, remember, she is struggling to breathe behind her mask of perfection. It's not easy being a joyful and capable woman, 24/7. Then there's innocent Betty. When Stella offered to help, Betty had no idea she was going to rope in Penny. But Betty had been overwhelmed when Paisley dropped off the roster, and it was a relief to have someone fill that need . . .

Far-fetched tale? I wish!

Really, this story is a compilation of just a few of the responses I received from Penny Loafers. It became clear that introverts in the church are often the ones most deeply wounded. I was grieved as I read testimonies of interventions, mean emails, phone calls, and even "eviction letters" telling women to leave the church—all because they are not recognized for the amazing, deep, thoughtful women they are.

You see, Loafers are listeners.

And typically, they are prayer warriors.

No, Pennys may not feel comfortable attending the women's retreats or functions, but they love the Lord fiercely, and if you are willing to talk to them, they can be the best friends you've ever had. It takes patience though. Talking to a Penny may be a bit uncomfortable at first, as they tend to not open up right away— especially if they have not yet been to the Cobbler for any needed repairs.

Let's examine a Loafer.

Unlike the *clickety–clack* of Stilettos, or the *clomping* of Boots, Loafers are almost silent as they move across the foyer floor. They're soft, pliable, and one of the most comfortable shoes around. You would never wear a Loafer to a ball, or to dig in a mucky garden. No, the Loafer is best worn for daily duties, where one needs to feel secure and steady on one's feet.

So then, why does it seem like the softest shoe is always the hardest hit?

I suggest it's because they are misunderstood and an easy target. Being so flexible, they often take on the criticism and demands of others, not fighting back or standing up for themselves. Their shyness is all too often labeled as being aloof or haughty. But how naughty are we who falsely judge these most dependable soles.

Let's hear from some of the walking wounded:

"I just attended a women's event at church this week and I stood there in a crowded room all alone. Ignored. Felt out of place. Uncomfortable. It felt like high school all over again. I stood at a table to see if a seat was available and I was just ignored while they carried on their conversation. Finally I spoke up asking if a seat was available. They said yes and then went back to their conversation, laughing and having a good time. All the while I'm sitting there at a table feeling awkward and unwelcomed. I finally moved seats, not like the next table was much better, but at least they acknowledged me when I sat."

~28-year-old American

"I still don't like to make connections with people I hardly know, but that is my own personality trait, not one fostered at the current church I attend."

~35-year-old Canadian

"I continue to search for a place of worship but I tend to lean toward more traditional, smaller locales where I find peace and closeness to God. I don't do well in large auditoriums or gyms—I find no peace or tranquility in those places."

~54-year-old Canadian

"One comment I would like to add is that I have experienced an 'all or nothing' attitude from these women (truth be told, there are a few men in there too!). The Nothings: some people have been absolutely oblivious to me, some have stood away from me chatting with their friends, obviously talking about me (determined by glances sent my way), and The Alls: some have overwhelmed me with their 'zealotry', so much so that it is uncomfortable to participate in a meaningful conversation with them. I have found more important, meaningful, God inspired conversation with women outside the church than in it!"

~50-year-old Canadian

"I've answered this in my wife's stead. I just can't get her to go to church. We've had many conversations about why, and it usually involves the fact that most women there are looking for any dirt they can get on a person, true or not; it makes no difference. And then they've GOT you. And they'll tolerate you out of the goodness of their huge hearts . . . But they treat you poorly in false grace. And if anyone has ever met and spent time with my lovely wife, they would know that there just is no dirt anywhere there to 'GET' on her. The woman is a saint."

~No age or country given

"I've been at my current church for two years now and still haven't made any really strong friendships. I love the ladies there, but they are all very established in their friendships and it makes it hard to break through."

~39-year-old American

"I kept to myself, not because I didn't want to be a part of the family of people at church, but I am shy in getting to know people and did feel that there were cliques within the ladies' groups that made me feel less inclined to interact."

~31-year-old British

"I have always been a Christian. But I am also an introvert . . . after two years, the pastor's wife—who I truly trusted and admired—all of the sudden approached me and again tried to convince me to go to her Bible study during the week. As an introvert I tend to dread these more intimate groups. I can talk and share in a one-on-one scenario but it's much harder for me to feel comfortable in a group. So I was always dodging that. But that day, the pastor's wife was determined to convince me otherwise. And during that talk I heard from her that I was selfish, that I wasn't growing in Christ, and that I have a problem and should look for professional help."

~38-year-old Australian

My word. We've done some vicious damage to our loyal, quiet Pennys.

Do you see yourself in these stories? Are you a limping Loafer? A punished Penny?

Or have you, in your frustration to round up volunteers or your earnest desire to see a Penny enter into fellowship, been the one who stomped on her sensitive toes?

It's going to be okay. We're going to take a walk to the Cobbler's shop soon and He, in His grace and mercy, can polish up any harsh scuffs we've caused or received. But we need to look out for our precious Pennys! They are such a treasure to the church and any group, particularly when we recognize and utilize their gift as a prayer cornerstone.

Let's peek a bit more into a Loafer's sole, shall we?

Loafers tend to feel like they don't belong, which is to be expected, as they are designed for solitude. But at the same time, Pennys want to be invited to things and feel like they belong . . . even if they probably won't attend. Yes, they would much rather be off somewhere alone. Loafers tend to be ultra-sensitive—often feeling judged and alienated, many are convinced that the "cool shoes" are standing in clumps talking about them, so be gracious and don't stare. Acknowledge Penny in a friendly, gentle way.

When approaching a Loafer, tread softly, and go alone. Typically, they prefer not to receive overwhelming hugs and loud greetings. In fact, a sincere smile and discreet wave across the room is usually heartwarming and sufficient, at least initially.

They love cards, texts, and emails, and will tolerate a quick call to say "hi" or to share a prayer request. However, we need to respect their wishes if they say they have to go. For a Penny, being stuck on the phone for longer than a few minutes is like having a foot with an ingrown toenail shoved in an undersized shoe.

In addition to prayer, seek their counsel. Many Pennys have the wisdom of Solomon tucked in their quiet little soles. Just be sure to let them process their thoughts. Give them time and space to mull—don't interrupt them when they are silent; they are contemplating and waiting on the Lord. Oh, and in case you're wondering, there is no such thing as awkward silence to a Loafer, unless you make it so.

Invite Penny over for coffee or tea, but don't be offended if she declines. Ask once in a while, but never to the point where she feels pressured. Loafers are soft structured shoes and easily squashed. It's not that she doesn't like you, she just enjoys her own space and doesn't need to spend a lot of time socializing. So do look for signs that she may be hurting or lonely and reach out, but respect her boundaries. She'll appreciate your caring words and understanding.

When a Penny is "stuck" in a large group setting where mingling is necessary, be sure to introduce her to people one-on-one and include her in your discussions. Don't expect her to chime in unless you specifically ask her something. Yes, she probably will stand there awkwardly, nodding her head occasionally and not uttering a word, but it will make her feel included and she will appreciate your sensitivity. Just don't grab her by the hand and pull her around introducing her to everyone in sight! (Oh, and she prefers to go to the women's washroom alone. Penny is not a "potty posse" girl).

Ah, sweet Penny Loafer. Now that you understand her a little bit more, don't you just love her? Can you even imagine what our churches would be like without her? Try and spot one next week, and then gently reach out to your shy sister. Who knows, she may just become your next best friend. In the meantime, won't you bow your head right where you are and ask the Lord to reveal if you have stepped on a loafer or two? Ask Him to forgive you and to give you courage to seek forgiveness from any Pennys you may have offended. And finally, that He would whisper a sense of belonging, wholeness, peace, joy and love into their quiet souls.

Penny? Are you still with us, dear?

Will you please forgive us louder—and sometimes insensitive—soles?

We don't mean to be so obtuse, but we are.

Are you doing okay?

We may not always hear you, but we do see you. We are beginning to get you more and more, and in fact, a few of us (make that a lot of us) could really use a friend like you. Keep praying for us, sister. We sure need it!

We love and appreciate you and your loyal, quiet sole.

4

Paisley Pump

Never let the brand name on your shoes be
more important than the ONE who's guiding
your footsteps.

Gracing the hallways and foyers of every church are
women who feel so insignificant, so ignored, that they believe they
are as invisible as the Emperor's new clothes.

Introducing Paisley Pump, a sensible yet sensitive sole who
only serves to beautify our fellowship walls. At least, that is how
she sees herself . . . as a church wallflower . . .

Paisley stared down at her cell phone, shocked at how
Betty had taken the news. When she saw the new shift schedule
last night, Paisley knew she wouldn't be able to assist consistently
with children's church. Gosh, how she hated letting people down.

After years of attending the church, Paisley only recently
found the courage to step out and join a ministry team. She not
only wanted to find a way to serve, but to make a few real
friendships as well. Maybe even have coffee with someone outside

of the church walls. Was that such a crazy idea? She spent time with work friends, but rarely hung out with any ladies from the fellowship, even though she made a point to connect with a few of them during the week via Facebook, email, text and sometimes a phone call. It seemed that everyone—including herself—had full calendars making face-to-face time hard to schedule.

Paisley recalled how excited and thankful Betty had been when she started to volunteer two months ago.

Two months ago, I was an answer to prayer. Today, I'm . . . a problem.

Betty is right, I am a flake.

The lump in her throat felt suffocating as she swallowed hard, taking in and embracing each unkind, hurtful word Betty had spoken.

Paisley had watched her for years, and even worked alongside her setting up a couple of summer barbeques. Betty was a solid woman of God. It just wasn't like her to say what she had said. *Clearly, I have thrown the poor girl into a dither.* Paisley's mouth twisted in dismay. *What is wrong with me? I should know by now that whenever I try to help or contribute, I end up messing up. I've got to make things right and apologize ASAP.*

Peeling off her hot, sticky uniform, Paisley dropped it into the hamper and turned on the shower, fiddling with the broken tap to set a comfortable temperature. She was exhausted after her graveyard shift, but couldn't imagine missing another Sunday. She had been on day shifts the last two weekends, and with the new rotation, she would be missing the next two Sundays as well. As tough as it was to accept the extra shifts and crazy new schedule, Paisley knew she had no choice. Her issues were nothing compared to what her co-worker, Julie, was going through. A second-time cancer patient, Julie looked like she was losing the battle. All her fellow workers had agreed to rally around Julie to cover her hours, then donate their overtime pay to help fund part of her medical bills and other needs.

The thought of the team uniting around Julie made Paisley smile, and helped her forget Betty's words for a moment. *That's just what family does. So thankful for my work family!*

Stepping into the shower, Paisley closed her eyes and let her heart be soothed by the mix of warm water running down her back and the worship music playing through her smartphone. Despair washed away as she rested in Him. Grabbing her favorite scented hair conditioner, she quickly lathered her legs to remove a weeks' worth of dark stubble.

Leaning against the wall of the shower to steady herself, she shuddered when she caught her reflection in the mirror directly across the glass shower doors. *What sick, twisted mind designed this bathroom?*

With the fur on her legs taken care of, Paisley turned and bravely faced the mirror, warm water still pummeling her. Turning slowly left to right she frowned at the reflection, allowing her hands to slowly work down her full figure, pausing here and there to grab at excess. She pushed the flesh this way and that as she stood sideways, sucking in her tummy. *Paisley, mercy, girl. Look at you . . . what happened? You're such a glutton.*

The praise-filled peace she had enjoyed only moments before flowed down the drain. With a heavy heart, Paisley flipped off the shower. She had taken way too long and now there was no time for primping. She dried off quickly, threw on a slip dress and grabbed the only pair of girl shoes she owned—beige, two-inch heeled, faux patent leather pumps—and ran out the door.

Making it just in time to get one of the last decent parking spots, Paisley steadied her pumps on the uneven gravel. When she heard worship start with *Amazing Grace,* she momentarily forgot she wasn't in her low, uniform shoe and broke out into a run. Well, as much as a lady can run in a dress while carrying a purse, Bible, and coffee.

Not a good idea.

Like a scene from a slow motion movie, Paisley saw one shoe rise in an arched trajectory in front of her, bounce a few times, then come to a skidding stop.

Hopping with painstaking effort, she picked up the runaway pump, and grimaced at the long, thick, black mark the sharp pebbles had left along one side. Sliding the shoe back on, she continued in a safer trot toward the side entrance doors, where she slipped into the sanctuary before the first verse was over.

Paisley craned her neck, checking Betty's spot in the back row again and again. Betty had an unofficial designated seat that allowed her to make a discreet exit right before the kids were dismissed for children's church. Paisley planned to scoot back and give her a quick hug of encouragement. She needed to make things right.

But today, the seat was empty.

I broke Betty. All because of my own stupidity!

When the hymn came to an end, Paisley took one last look back and was relieved to see Betty walk through the door. Pump's relief was short-lived, though, when she saw who was with her—Stella. Paisley watched in discomfort as Stella gave Betty a quick squeeze before parting.

Betty slid into her pew, not making eye contact with anyone. And Stella—well, she strode forward, in her confident-woman-walk, to her usual spot in the front row. For a second, Paisley's eyes met Stella's. *Is it my imagination, or did she just give me a squinty stink-eye?*

Hunkering down in her pew, Paisley was certain Betty had told Stella what a flake she was. *Oh great. Now I've got to worry about Stella too. The one woman I sometimes wish didn't know my name!*

After five years attending the church, it wasn't until recently that Paisley believed anyone even knew her name. In fact, when registering for her umpteenth women's event last month, the gal behind the table tried to cover up for not knowing her by asking how to spell her last name, as she "always gets it wrong".

"P. U. M. P. —you know—like the shoe?"

Caught in her blunder, the registrar was mortified, but Paisley just laughed and spent the rest of the event loving on the woman. She was certain the registrar was beating herself up for thinking she had upset her. Paisley wasn't offended, but she was sure the well-intentioned woman thought she had—a tormenting mindset that Paisley understood all too well.

Still down low in her seat, Paisley glanced around the sanctuary, taking stock of who was there and who was away. Most of the regular faces were present, but she noticed Mona was missing again. She hadn't seen her in weeks, but then Paisley had been away a fair amount, too, so maybe they were just missing each other. Still, she wondered. Mona appeared to be really struggling the last few times they spoke.

Paisley pulled out her cell and set a reminder to call Mona that day, after her much-needed Sunday nap.

So many women are hurting. No one seems to be thriving or growing.

From the corner of her eye, she saw Cindy. *Gosh! I've had her birthday card in my purse for weeks. She probably thinks I forgot about her.* With a sickening feeling in her stomach, Paisley dug inside her purse, pulling out the pouch that held all her miscellaneous cards and such. Quietly, she unzipped the bag and thumbed through tattered outreach brochures and five dollar coffee cards she gave to the homeless. Wedged in-between, she found the small, bent-up envelope containing the birthday greeting. She flattened her purse on the pew next to her and placed the card on top.

Today . . . it was going to end up in that amazing girl's hands.

Today . . . I am going to make amends with several people and ask forgiveness.

Today . . . I am going to redeem all kinds of wrongs!

Oh sensitive, slightly paranoid, Paisley. If shoes had antennae, her pair would be three feet long. Much like the character, Radar, from the show *M*A*S*H*, Paisley keeps her eyes and ears tuned in to whatever is happening amongst the churchwomen. No, not because she's a gossip, but because she actually *feels* each person's aches and breaks.

So who exactly is this Pump sole, anyway?

While not nearly as quiet as Penny Loafers, Paisleys nevertheless are practically invisible. They are rarely heard coming and going by those around them. *Or at least, that's how they feel.* A bit introverted, they tend to hang back against our church foyer walls, taking everything in. No sling-backs or open toes for Pumps, as they are carrying way too much of a load to leave themselves vulnerable to slippage. Their sensible heels allow them to move quickly to minister to a lonely woman—which they do quite often.

But their soles are also sensitive. Not just tender to those around them . . . they are also vulnerable to penetration by sharp words and actions.

Yes, Pumps are a functional shoe—tougher than a loafer, but softer than a boot—so their pliability often results in many scuffs and smears.

Surprisingly though, Paisleys walk as if their feet are steady and sure. They desire to dash in and rescue whomever they can. You could say they're a bit of a shoe-closet superhero! If cloning were possible, Paisleys would want to go on the waitlist. They would love nothing more than to be able to reach out to every new shoe walking in the door, while at the same time, following up with the gals met weeks before. Their hearts are focused on making sure nobody falls through the cracks.

You see, a Pump is a behind-the-scenes people "fixer". She is a stealthy lover of all.

Maybe people don't remember her name. Maybe she doesn't get invited out very often . . . but she impacts people much more than she knows. Her caring, soft touch, offer of prayer or a word of encouragement—these things matter. A lot.

Let's hear from our "invisible" friends so we can better understand them:

"Have been longing to find a sense of community. The church is already an established group and no opening for possible new connections. I do go out of my way to speak to people who stand on their own, and record their names and minor details to hopefully respond to when I meet them again."

~No age or country given

"The cliques of other women at church. Don't necessarily want to break into their circles, but at the same time feel very left out. We've been at our current church for a year–and–a–half and still no friends I can talk with during the week. Too many 'established' friendships already set in place, so seems not much room for new ones. I will keep persevering and praying!"

~No age or country given

"I attend a church. I have heard from others that our church is very friendly. I DON'T feel it. That being said, I also think, I too have inflicted pain on others."

~38-year-old American

". . . with moving many times over the years and attending new churches, I have always found (women especially) have their own group of friends, and it is generally hard to be included in these groups. People get too wrapped up in their own longtime friendship groups (cliques) and neglect to welcome newcomers, which is sad!"

~75-year-old, no country given

"So many women have more activities on their plate and also work. Finding the time, then taking time to get involved in women ministry, is not the top of their priority. So grateful [for] the women who have patience and persistence with me."

~No age or country given

"I love going to church and I love the ladies. I hope and pray I don't exclude anyone. It is too easy to feel comfortable. I try not to miss seeing someone's needs for comfort or encouragement. What a blessing it is to be a blessing to others. We/I should pray for more of a compassionate heart to love others as Jesus loves. Blessings!"

~72-year-old Australian

"I attended about four women's retreats with our church and thought I would be able to make a few friends, but most times I came home not wanting to go to another retreat as the women were too cliquey (they had their own groups and I was the odd woman out)."

~44-year-old Canadian

"It's a curious thing that women tend not to speak up over actual moral issues, but like to pick people apart/ignore them over the non-moral. It seems it's easy in women's groups for ladies to shut other ladies out because they don't dress 'fashionably', or have an 'overly' boisterous personality, or a 'too' shy personality. As a youth leader, I feel discouraged that girls (and boys, too) sometimes seem to prefer the company of their cell phones over other people. And like the women, the girls want to appear 'normal' to everyone. It's hard to find people who are willing to stand out to follow Jesus—which is an ancient problem that I'm not expecting to be done away with any time soon! :)"

~19-year-old American

"I have heard it said, 'we have the right to pick our friends'. I strongly disagree. I have surrendered my rights to the King of Kings. He chooses my friends. Once I realized I was part of the problem, feeling sorry for myself for not being with the 'in group' of ladies at my church, and asked God to pick my friends . . . it's amazing what happened . . . I have friends, great ones. I was missing out on amazing women who needed me as much as I needed them. Before I was a Christian I was in a sorority where they picked you based on how pretty you were, your GPA, how 'cool' you were. Oh I am afraid it's in the church as well. Lord call us out, to be set apart. Let us love . . . period."

~No age or country given

Amen Paisley! Preach it, sister!

How sad that Pumps describe themselves as "average" women and "invisible".

Perhaps vanilla would be another adjective.

Yet as I write this, I think about my own crazy footwear collection. I have several pairs of stilettos, including both a giraffe and a zebra print I picked up at a consignment store for a dollar a pair. I have at least six pairs of soft, flat, loafer-like shoes. I also have about three different styles of snow boots, but live in a climate that maybe sees two days of recordable snowfall a year. Flip-flops? Oh, I'd estimate no less than six pairs—a few flat ones, a couple with small heels, two pairs of ridiculously tall platform beach slides . . .

But the pair of shoes that I adore . . . that I LOVE . . . are my sensible, beige, woven, two-inch heeled pumps. I wear them to almost every wedding, and take them on absolutely every business trip. I have had them restored, cleaned, and resoled *several times* by a professional cobbler.

I paid twenty-five dollars for them over six years ago at a consignment shop.

My cobbler bills must be at least four times that amount by now.

But they are *my* shoe. They are so worth the investment.

There is something to be said for a soft, comfortable, safe yet stylish shoe that seems to go with everything. But with that pliability comes vulnerability. My favorites have taken some brutal blows. They've had some deep, black marks that I was sure would never come out. They also have had some damage on the inside— something only I knew about.

Fortunately, with professional help, they were restored every time—inside and out—in part because I didn't neglect them too long.

But back to our slightly-paranoid Paisley. Like all of us, she gets her share of bruises and knocks. Yet, so focused on everyone else, she often tends to ignore the damage to herself. She goes on and on in her giving, without noticing the personal cost. There are layers that need to be pulled back and tended to by The Cobbler. Oh how we all need that from time to time, and when we do sit with Him for a bit, it's awesome to see our soles restored!

So, are you a Paisley? Do you feel invisible, and yet at the same time believe almost everyone is judging you? Do you apologize often and find yourself constantly trying to make amends?

Maybe this is not you, but it describes one of your best friends . . . if so, please recognize she is struggling and needs some fixin's to her sole . . . show her grace!

Gosh, one of my Paisley seasons was *brutal*.

I interpreted almost everything wrong, which is not surprising, as I was tuned into everything. Imagine turning on your television, radio, a YouTube podcast, and then sitting down with a book and trying to focus on all of them at the same time. That's the best that I can explain what my beige, insignificant, frustrating existence was like. The irony of believing yourself to be insignificant, yet also thinking that everything is about you, is not lost on me. If you've never lived this, trust me, it happens to many of us, and is usually due to unresolved issues and unhealed wounds.

We Pumps can be a cracked shoe.

In my case, the Cobbler needed to peel back layer after layer until He was able to work on the inner hurts, some of which went back to childhood abuse. Not a pretty picture, but that's where it started with me—and no doubt, for many of you.

Again, does Paisley's story resonate with you? When you walk through the foyer, do you feel everyone's emotions sticking to your soul? And perhaps more than just sticking to you, are your own emotions sometimes rubbed raw?

Like me, are you in much need of The Cobbler's touch? Do you interpret problems and issues going on around you as all being your fault?

56

A few women are chatting over in the corner? Paisley is sure they are talking about her unfashionable heel height . . .

The women's ministry director and another woman go behind closed doors? Paisley is sure it's because of something she's done.

In fact, the only thing worse than what Paisley thinks people are saying about her, is what she is saying to herself.

Paisleys rarely see or remember the good things they have done. Perhaps it's because these sensitive soles are often lost in the back of their closets, buried deep beneath a pile of shoulda, coulda, and wouldas!

I shoulda done more . . . I coulda done that better . . . I woulda spent more time . . . if only.

Pumps are often so hard on themselves.

Hear us Paisley—you are amazing!

You bring light and the fragrance of Christ into so many women's lives.

Your ability to remember names and dates is astounding. Your gentle touch and encouraging words have given quiet hope to many women who felt alone and forgotten.

Your friendship is a gift from The Cobbler.

We other soles need to recognize Pumps when we come across them in our foyers. If you have a sensitive friend who apologizes to inanimate objects, criticizes herself incessantly, and has frantic "fix" reminders all over her calendar . . . she's most likely in her Pump season.

Gently, lovingly, remind her that she doesn't need to apologize as much as she does—everything is not her fault. Lead her to the Cobbler. I remember signing up for a special Bible study because I knew if I didn't go, neither would a friend of mine—and she really needed help! At the time, I didn't believe *I* needed the small group, but I was wrong. Turns out, I needed to be cobbled, as much if not more than my friend. Of course, in the end, both of us had our shoes and socks blessed off!

Let's take a moment, close our eyes and pray for our peacemaking, sensitive Pump friends. Perhaps we can take a moment on Sunday to look along our church walls and pick out a few wallflowers to love on. We need to call our Paisleys by name, acknowledge their friendship, and invite a Pump or two out for coffee, or better yet, into our homes and lives.

And you, Paisley . . . my empathetic, deep-feeling, sister Pump. I have lived in your sensitive sole!

Relax. Breathe. Wiggle your toes for a moment and let your lungs expand deep into your diaphragm. You may *feel* unseen, but you are seen. You may not *feel* like many people care for you, but we do. You are loved. You are so needed and appreciated. The Cobbler made you, and He doesn't make mistakes.

Please know the way you interpret and see the world is not as bad as you think. Like every shoe, Pumps are only seasonal footwear. I pray that you periodically slip out of your shoes and spend some time with the Cobbler. Perhaps it's time to be examined, cleaned, and resoled before stepping out again or trying on a new style . . . but then again, isn't that's true for all of us?

5

Mona Misfit

I walk slowly . . . but I never walk backwards.

~Abe Lincoln

Have you ever had the misfortune of getting to your destination, only to realize that you're wearing two different shoes? With no time to spare, you're forced to go throughout your lopsided day as though colorblind.

Welcome, would you, Mona Misfit!

Mona is not only keenly aware of her compromised condition, but actually struggles day after day in mismatched soles.

Mona lay in her bed frustrated. Once again, she had missed church. Would she ever adjust to this "new normal"?

As tears welled up, she flipped over and bit her pillow to muffle her cry. Mona's husband did not need to see her lose it yet again. Harry was having his own struggles.

For Mona, this relapse was different than any she had experienced previously. Everything hurt. There appeared to be no relief. Even the light touch of the bed sheets caused her to want to cry out in pain. She was sick and tired of being . . . sick and tired.

Sitting up, she winced when her soft, cotton nighty caught under her thigh.

Lord, heal me or take me.

Mona let her bare feet hit the floor, not even considering wearing her slippers. In fact, if she weren't so self-conscious, she would choose to be in her birthday suit all day. What a riot that would be when the kids showed up for Sunday dinner!

Just as she was awkwardly trying to rise to her feet, Harry appeared with coffee and the usual handful of morning pills.

"Honey, you're up!"

"You . . . wet me . . . sweep in . . ." Mona enunciated the best she could.

"We had a bad night, babe. I didn't think you could handle sitting through the service." Harry gently rubbed her back, and Mona flinched, trying not to let the discomfort show. "If we get ready . . . we could still make it," he continued hesitantly.

Hope stirred in Mona's tired bones. She smiled up at him; words were not necessary. By the time they'd arrive at church, Mona figured her painkillers would have taken off the edge and she would be able to just take it all in . . .

With hubby's assistance, Mona dressed quickly. It wasn't until Harry was assisting her into her wheelchair in the church parking lot that she realized she was wearing two different shoes. She glanced into the car, but there was no lap blanket to hide her feet.

Tucking the foot with the sparkling, black flat behind her other leg, she allowed the dark–green loafer to take predominance on the footrest.

Good grief! What a day! But no matter, I'm home.

The sound of her favorite hymn, *Amazing Grace*, could be heard. She smiled and gave Harry yet another silent signal. Oh, how she loved that song. Her weight shifted as the chair jerked its way through the unforgiving gravel. Having arrived a bit late, all the paved handicapped spots were filled. Her husband grunted under the strain as Mona struggled to stay upright. Her lips pursed tightly as they rolled past young, able-bodied Cindy's car parked in the handicapped section.

My, these inconsiderate youth. Lord, protect my man and give him an added measure.

Finally, in the safe sanctuary, Harry and Mona took a moment to regroup and breathe after the winding ramp up to the door. Physically, it was hard on both of them. Mona felt every jar and lurch.

The last verse of her song was still being sung, and they waited—eyes closed—taking in the presence of the Lord. It was comforting medicine for their tired bones.

When the song ended, Mona opened her eyes to show her mate of 32 years that she was ready to head into the sanctuary.

An elder opened the heavy door so that Harry could manage the chair with a little more ease. Mona looked up to thank the kind young elder, but he nervously broke eye contact, clearing his throat and checking his watch.

It's not contagious you know . . . but as soon as the negative thought came, Mona took it captive and shut it down. She did look a sight—unmatched shoes, wrinkled clothes, and sitting slightly crooked in her chair. *Most people,* she imagined, *must think I'm a simpleton or something given the way I speak and sometimes drool.*

I may be a misfit, but I'm His misfit, and God is not face palming at my condition. Jesus loves me, and I love Him, and that's what matters most—even more than Harry.

Closing her eyes, Mona smiled as the worship songs washed over her. No longer able to sing along, the words of each hymn saturated her soul as she sat smiling a tender, crooked grin. Suddenly, the voice of the assistant pastor broke through as he began to review the week's announcements. Opening her eyes, Mona saw Paisley Pump waving at her from her usual spot.

Dear, complicated, wonderful Paisley. She never seems uncomfortable around me at all. She even calls me sometimes during the week, which is amazing as I'm quite certain she can't always understand my mispronounced words. Still, when Paisley's around, I actually feel . . . useful . . . and dare I say . . . normal?

Ms. Pump would often come and kneel next to Mona's chair. Leaning in, she would enquire about Harry and Mona's week, and then often ask for advice and biblical counsel. *It is as if my wheelchair, my slurred words . . . are . . . invisible to her!*

Mona gave Paisley a slight wave of acknowledgement, then turned her attention to Stella Stiletto, who was working her way up the short set of stairs toward the podium. *Would you look at those gorgeous heels!* Suddenly self-conscious of her own unstylish, mismatched soles, Mona tucked the black shoe even tighter behind her other leg.

"Ladies and gentlemen, this coming Saturday, we are celebrating Valentine's Day at the go-kart tracks. This year, we're going to tally run times and have husbands competing against their wives. There is something for *everybody*, so come on out and join in the fun. I expect to see you all there!" Giving the congregation a dramatic wink, and miming an imaginary steering wheel, Stella made her way back down to her front row seat.

Mona smiled and prayed to herself. *Lord, thank you for that young wife and mother. Give her strength and encouragement as she leads us— her motley crew. Grace upon grace for that gal, dear Jesus. Grace upon grace.*

Years ago, before the disease began its cruel damage, Mona was often judgmental and critical of Stella. Now, being shut in and with more time in the Word and prayer, God had begun a change in her heart. You see, in her younger years, Mona liked to wear ridiculously high heels herself. She was quite the leader in her time. When she stepped down and passed the leadership to the new generation, she gave Mrs. Stiletto a bit of a hard time during the transition. She'd point out each and every blunder and stumble. And this terrible attitude wasn't just toward Stella, but everyone.

For instance, Betty Boot. Mona was never a fan of her gregarious nature, or her sticky, overcooked meals, but boy . . . she had a different view of her now. Betty hadn't said a word to anyone at church about her mom's terminal illness, but Mona found out during one of her own late-night ER visits. Hospitals make for thin walls and few secrets. Yet, with all that was happening with her mom, Betty still showed up every Tuesday with a cheerful smile and hot, nutritious food for her and Harry. Not one to let Mona off the hook when it came to ministry, Betty "kept her in the game" by always including a few *Jesus Knows Your Name* booklets, with a note encouraging the Misfits to witness and minister. While some may have found that presumptuous, it made Mona feel as though Betty believed she could still be used—even in her compromised state.

Lord, bless them both, and thank You for changing my heart.

Mona felt her head tilting to one side. As she struggled to straighten it out, Penny Loafer smiled sweetly from across the aisle, but then dropped her gaze.

My shy, quiet prayer warrior. Mona watched her lips move slowly, and knew that she was lifting her up in prayer, as she supposed Penny did often. No sooner had she entertained the thought when newfound strength surged into her neck and limbs. She smiled, straightening a little, supported by her Father's touch.

God, yes indeed, thank you for these women. Bless them—all of them, Jesus—and I pray I can continue to be a blessing to them. Even in this broken, mismatched, misfit state of mine.

Oh, Mona Misfit! She is so alienated in her shut-off world. If Pumps are invisible, and Loafers are silent . . . Misfits and Mismatches are both. Struggling with health issues, (sometimes visible, sometimes not), their feet often rest on wheelchair footrests, and don unused, unworn soles. They quietly roll down our church halls and foyers, all too often unacknowledged. Sadly, Monas are fully aware of their lack of a "normal" *clickety-clack, stomp,* or *shuffle.*

No, like a beautiful bride, Mona, you *swoosh* in the Spirit!

Caregivers and a handful of intuitive, patient friends are blessed beyond measure with the depth of love and knowledge that Monas hide in their unmarked soles. So often, the rest of us shoes may wrongfully think Misfits have nothing to contribute . . . or we are paralyzed in fear and uncertainty, not knowing how to relate to or appreciate these godly soles.

So we look away.

Or nod, but keep walking.

Or we give our Misfits a wide berth, sometimes crossing the foyer to avoid the awkwardness.

My, oh my, how we inflict pain without laying a hand or word on them. In fact, it's our lack of touch that can make Mismatches and Misfits hurt more than we know.

Let's hear from a few, shall we?

"I find my face doesn't correctly portray what I'm feeling. Sometimes I wonder if sagging jowls with age make people think I'm scowling when actually I'm just thinking. Check-out clerks get wide-eyed, and if I realize what's happening, I'll smile and speak, which usually helps. I do wonder how many people have gained the wrong impression without my realizing it."

~Over 65, no country given

"Men and women in the church are very good at sticking to their own connections, and whilst are friendly enough on a Sunday or in a home group, all too often we are not very good at extending that hand of friendship further. I am an immigrant in a new country with no family over here, and it is extremely difficult to take relationships further than the Sunday. I have recently been diagnosed with depression, which I have told some other people, and not one of them has contacted me in the week to see how I am doing. But as you say, we are flawed, and this is where Jesus has led my family to, and I know that I need to work on inviting people into my life better . . ."

~No age given, British

"As a person with a physical disability (had polio), and a wheelchair user, I often feel ignored and of little value. Physical appearance seems to be the 'accepting' criteria. However, I know my value in God's eyes and am comfortable with who I am.
I am often targeted by many as an object needing healing, rather than the person being concerned with other needs I might have.
Sometimes when people approach me, usually unasked, and want to pray for me, I often reply 'What do you have in mind exactly?' which makes them think, what did they have in mind, my healing, their glory, their non-acceptance of me as I am, in a wheelchair."

~68-year-old New Zealander

"I had (an illness) . . . and since then I have suffered with bad breath and body odour on and off . . . but I have really struggled with being around people because of it, and so most of the isolation is my own fault, but I find that a lot of people at church won't sit near me, and don't really approach me to chat. Again, I'm most likely giving off negative vibes by my trying to protect myself from rejection, but I just don't feel comfortable at church or feel like I can open up to anyone. I have opened up to my pastor and his wife and they have counselled me, but I'm terribly lonely and isolated, God has been my rock and comfort."

~40-year-old Irish

"When I brought a personal situation to the woman's ministry lead, she told me 'Maybe this is God's way of saying you should just go home to your family. If you were following His Will, this wouldn't have happened.' All I heard was 'This was your fault that this happened to you, just go running home and admit your failure. You obviously did something to deserve this'."

~30-year-old American

"I was ignored by my own pastor when my brother had a freak allergic reaction that put him in a coma. No one from church called to ask how we were doing, how he was. When I came back to church after my brother was released from the hospital, it was like nothing had ever happened. Just this past year my daughter was hospitalized and the doctors didn't think she was going to make it. Some of the women prayed for us but no one told our pastor what happened. He called me, crying, saying how bad he felt that we were ignored, and this time not intentionally."

~34-year-old American

Can we take a moment, right now, and lift up these hurting Monas to the Lord?

Father, You are El Roi—the God Who Sees—and You are also Jehovah Rapha—the God Who Heals. We ask You, then, to pour out Your Spirit upon these women. Wherever they are, may they sense Your power, Your healing, and Your presence. Forgive us for avoiding the very ones that You died for. Help us to see past their issues and into their precious souls. Change our hearts so that we would naturally reach out in love and acceptance. May we be Your eyes, ears, hands, and feet on this broken earth. In Jesus' name, Amen.

Do you sometimes feel like a misfit? Does what people see not truly reflect what's going on inside of you? Are you struggling with the discomfort of that misfitting sole? If so, forgive us, sister, for our own short-sightedness and ignorance.

This footwear encompasses a large group of women with all kinds of various issues that often keep people at arm's distance. Mona's are avoided as other shoes don't know what to say or how to help. Sticky topics such as sickness, financial difficulties, wayward or struggling children stop us in our tracks. Too often, our awkwardness results in us totally ignoring them or, as Betty feared, giving them the dreaded pity head-tilt.

Perhaps you feel more like a mismatched sole. Do you have one foot in one style and the other in another? Are you a *clickety-shuffle*? Or an invisible *clomp*? Perhaps you're like our friend Mona and exhibit a *clickety-swoosh-shuffle*.

You see, while physically limited, Mona can and does still lead. She is living out her season with Psalm 71:18 coming to fruition in her life: *"so even to old age and gray hairs, O God, do not forsake me, until I proclaim your might to another generation, your power to all those to come."*

Mona may not be able to navigate in six-inch heels anymore, but you bet that she's still leading with a confident *clickety-clack* in a few people's lives. She listens without judgment, and proclaims His might with her gray-haired wisdom.

With so much time in bed, she fills her quiet hours praying over the needs of her family, her church, her nation and the many women in her life. *Shuffle-shuffle.*

Finally, with humble submission to God, and tired of her long, anger-filled battle, Mona let go of the frustration of her incomplete physical healing. She knows God's touch, and has felt His hand many times over the last few months. He can, and does heal, but for whatever reason, her full external healing has not come. But her internal healing—that's another story. Over time as she sat with The Cobbler, He healed many of her old hurts and Mona drew closer and closer to Him. So much in so little time, and in such unexpected ways. And now, full to the measure with the Holy Spirit, Mona is fine with rolling instead of running. She has His Perfect Peace.

Swoosh!

Oh that I could be swooshing in the Spirit more consistently.

Not too long ago, I was sick with pneumonia and had to drag myself to a walk-in clinic for a prescription. As I swung my legs out of the car, I realized I had worn two different shoes. Oh the horror. On registering my name, I was told it would be forty-five minutes before I would see a doctor, so I hobbled back to the car to hide my foot shame. Surely if I saw my blunder, the whole world must be pointing and snickering.

Of course they weren't. Everyone in the waiting room was as broken as I was, and they probably felt self-conscious about their own junk. Red, snotty noses, an oozy bandaged toe peeking out from a pair of flip-flops, and on the other side of the room, a barf bucket sat on a lap.

But my unmatched shoes—now that was embarrassing!

I'd like to say I rose above it and was secure in who I was in Christ like Mona, but I've gotta tell ya, I buckled. Unwashed hair, wrinkled clothes . . . my mismatched feet were the last straw. My man came riding in on his white stallion (or quite possibly an old blue F-150) and brought me two matching sets. (A gal always needs a choice.)

As I wrote Mona Misfit's story, I kept that uncomfortable, silly day in mind. If I could be so self-conscious with a ridiculously minor fashion infraction, how must these beautiful women feel when their physical, mental, or emotional states are so mismatched from who they know they truly are?

Are you a Mona, hobbling or rolling in our halls with different shoes?

Mercy. I can't even imagine the vulnerability and frustration you must feel. Forgive us, kind ladies, for our social ineptness. May the Lord help us get past our own insecurities so we would be able to reach out and get to know you. You have so much to offer us—starting with deep, meaningful friendship.

Or maybe you don't have physical issues, but nonetheless *feel* like a misfit? That situation can be so crushing to soles. Sometimes you may feel unworthy to even come to church and be with others. After all, everyone else, unlike you, have their stuff together. *Or so you think.* Let me assure you, there have been many times when my mask showed a contented woman living a wonderful life, but in reality, there was an emotional hurricane wreaking havoc in my heart. I faked it pretty good. So many of us do! The truth is we are all broken in one way or another, and to some extent, will remain so until we take up permanent residence with the Cobbler. In other words, you are not alone.

Mona, how do you see yourself? And how does your heavenly Father see you? These two viewpoints should be the same. If not . . . not to worry; there is help to be found. There is healing under our Cobbler's hands. Not always as we would hope, nor in our desired timing, but mercy, how He loves you and wants to heal your inner hurts and use you.

And as for the rest of us, by now, you've walked a mile in some of our shoes and have seen that none of us are stepping in perfect rhythm. We're all stumbling, getting stepped on, stepping on others, and along the way, a few may have even lost a shoe.

6

Cindy Solo

If you don't think shoes are important, just
ask Dorothy & Cinderella!

With my slightly warped sense of humor, I often muse when I see a lone, abandoned shoe in the middle of the road. How exactly did that happen? And when did the poor gal realize she was missing something?

Hello Cindy Solo! This is one shoe who is very aware that she is "missing" a mate. Not that it's always a big deal to her—but it sure is to those around her! *At least, that's what she thinks . . .*

Cindy pulled into the church parking lot a bit too fast, sending gravel flying up behind her sporty convertible. Having made it with only a few minutes to spare, she was rather relieved there was still one handicapped parking spot available. *Whew. Today, I qualify as being handicapped.*

Opening her door, she rested her swollen left foot on the jam and adjusted the tension bandage, grimacing at the sight of black and blue extending down to her toes. It looked so nasty, she couldn't believe it wasn't broken. *Ah, makes for a great story to tell. A battle wound to be proud of. Who knew that community volleyball could result in such drama?*

Checking her cell phone, Cindy decided she had a minute to post a graphic shot of the injury on her social media feed.

"I guess this is an example of victory in de-feet!" she captioned. *"Dove to save the final ball, giving us victory—but at the expense of my ankle. So worth it!"*

Dropping the phone into her purse, her comment reminded her of a favorite quote from John F. Kennedy—one she had memorized for a school presentation years ago . . . 'Victory has a thousand fathers, but defeat is an orphan'.

Gosh, since moving here ten years ago, there are a lot of days when I feel like an orphan. Ten years! And to think, not one person from church remembered my birthday this year. Not one . . .

Just as she was hunkering down in her own pity party, a comforting verse came to mind, shutting it down.

"I will not leave you as orphans; I will come to you." (John 14:18)

She shook off the melancholy and grabbed her crutches from the empty passenger seat. Holding them together with one hand, Cindy planted them on the pavement and leveraged her weight easily out of the car. This was not her first sports injury, as she was known for her gusto and dedication all through high school and college. "If you're going to commit to something, be all in," was the motto she would reiterate to her teammates at practices. Almost always the team captain, everyone would say what a natural leader she was and what a great mother she'd be.

Someday.

Someday never came for Cindy—at least not yet. But, just like during a game, she knew it wasn't over until it was over. So she waited. Kind of.

Hopping on the crutches toward the sanctuary door, Cindy felt her face flush when Daniel opened the heavy, wooden door for her. "What happened to you?" he asked, flashing his perfectly handsome smile.

"Well, Elder Daniel," Cindy said, flicking his black name badge in playful mockery, "wouldn't you like to know . . . you should see the other gal! Best watch your step! And by the way, how can someone younger than thirty be considered an elder? Who did you pay to get that title?"

Daniel's mouth dropped open as she turned and moved on toward the young adults' section. Halfway down the aisle, she stopped. *When exactly was one no longer considered a young adult?* Awkwardly, she forced herself to flop into an empty seat at the end of the nearest pew.

Gosh, Cindy. You're so weird. No wonder nobody asks you out; you're too outspoken and pushy. Poor Daniel. He looked so embarrassed by your comment. And what are you doing flirting the way you do? Don't you know this is church? Besides, not only are you too old for him, let's face it . . . you've got a past, girl. Nobody wants used goods. Why do you think no one calls you anymore? They probably all know . . .

Cindy closed her eyes, and as Stella had once taught her, tried to take every thought captive in an effort to shut up the barrage of words attacking her. She had fought this fight many times before. One minute she would be flying high and confident; the next, she was down for the count. Taking a few deep breaths, Cindy felt her shoulders relax as she silently repeated a few times to herself, *'there is no condemnation in Christ'*.

Thankfully, *'Amazing Grace'* soon filled her ears and displaced the void in her soul. Oh, how she loved praise and worship!

The singing ended far too soon, interrupted by the dreaded announcements. Cindy dug in her purse, looking for a candy or mint. Suddenly she heard Stella's voice break the mundane male's monologue. She sat up, waiting expectantly. This was always fun. Then ...

Valentine's Day? Oh just kill me already.

She looked around at the group of people most would call "church family". But she didn't feel like a real member . . . no, she was definitely an orphan. If true connection hadn't happened after ten years, maybe it was time to look elsewhere to be "adopted". She knew so many people, yet over the years, one by one, they had all been matched up and married. It seemed like she was always a third, fifth, or seventh wheel. Old people kept nudging her at weddings saying, 'You just wait, Cindy . . . you'll be next!' Cindy had to bite her witty-tongue not to say the same thing to them at funerals. Of course she wouldn't . . . but that was just the way her sanguine, funny mind thought.

As for her church friends, slowly, the dinner and movie nights got harder and harder to coordinate as everyone was busy setting up homes and starting families.

Cindy had been left behind, feeling discarded and forgotten on her journey.

Dear Cindy. She came here to start a new life, but the dark secret she carries tends to control her. So now she keeps everyone at a safe distance, using her humor and fun personality as a shield.

She hops around our foyers, missing a piece of herself and her wardrobe. Cindy is all too aware of how she is different, and feels alienated and "not quite right" in her standing amongst the other women. Women who are fully functional and, of course, two-shoed. She's less than.

At least, that's how she sees herself.

How my heart breaks for Cindy! If only she could be free, once and for all, to walk in victory and see herself through the grace-filled eyes of her Savior. She is right about one thing, though.

There is therefore now no condemnation for those who are in Christ Jesus. For the law of the Spirit of life has set you free in Christ Jesus from the law of sin and death. (Romans 8:1-2)

Our bouncy Cindy Solo keeps taking a few hops forward in this truth, and then a few hops back when the enemy trips her. She "gets it" but doesn't "keep it".

Are you a single-slippered gal? Do you sometimes feel like you're missing something?

Too many women believe they will not be accepted if they attend church without a man at their side. Some even feel churches don't want them.

Let's hear from a few of our hopping friends:

"I started going to my current church because the pastor was my youth pastor at another church, and I wanted my kids to have that sense of belonging that the pastor created for me. Little did I know we would be treated like third class citizens! I was in college, a single mom raising three young kids. Married couples would not include me in their outings, even though I was married for many years and could have given some insight to some of the issues they were facing . . . Since joining this church, I got engaged and the married couples now talk to me. It is a strange phenomenon and I am sure I am not the only divorced single mom who has gone through a similar situation in church. Single divorced women and men are often left out of church groups and outings."

~34-year-old American

"Having grown up with parents that attended different churches, I now attend alone, as my husband is a non-believer. He is a wonderful, respectful man and we have a great relationship. It makes others at church uncomfortable. I would say that generally my biggest wound has been when people tell me they feel sorry for me because my whole family doesn't share the same beliefs . . . It is not that he doesn't believe, he is just unsure of which religion is right. He has always supported me in going and in introducing our children to religion. I have always felt that my religious upbringing has taught me great acceptance of many different views and to embrace the differences in our world. However, most churches don't know how to react to it and tend to leave me out of most things."

~50-year-old, no country given

"I'm a Christian feminist—this gets tricky when it comes to joining in fellowship among other Christian women. I have female friends that have been treated badly in church because of their sexual relationships with their boyfriends, and their boyfriends were never treated any differently. A church I occasionally attend has 'ladies luncheons' and while the women are wonderful, and very welcoming, there is a lot that is based on assumptions about women, that I'm really uncomfortable with—icebreakers like 'name as many cleaning products as you possibly can in two min with your table.' It just seems too old-fashioned to me."

~27-year-old Canadian

"I did attend a small church but was never included, and then separated because of a divorce, so then never fit in because I didn't have a husband, so wasn't considered to have a 'family'."

~47-year-old Canadian

"I attend a church but consider myself non-denominational. 'Jesus is my Saviour, not my religion' is my motto. I was born again three years ago and my past is very shady. I was open in my testimony but felt I had to tone it back a bit. Once saved you are accepted, and when baptism followed, I felt accepted. Some ladies just don't have the kind of past that some of us have and really can't understand it. I feel the Pastor sets the tone of the church and we have a fairly new one after twelve months turmoil, so we'll see. I always stay for tea after the service and this helps. The cliques happen if some 'serve' more than others, but I was determined to follow through my walk with the Lord."

~60-year-old Australian

Oh, our limping, mate-less sweethearts!

How sad to think about them, hopping around on one foot, feeling left out of the paired-up congregation. I know quite a few Cindys who have never been married and are quite happy and content in their single status . . . except many of them do feel alienated.

How do we view singles in our church family? Do we include them in our outings and activities? Is what they feel true? Or is it just another of Satan's deceptions?

I fear it's both.

I walked as a Solo following a divorce. I not only lost my mate, but had my vulnerable, exposed foot stomped on by many Christians—both male and female. It was a horrible, hard time. I believed divorcing my husband meant I also had to divorce Jesus. I was wrong . . . so wrong, but that is what I believed. It took some time, but eventually I knew that God loved me, and I needed to seek Him again.

Even while knowing His love, limping back into a church as a single mom was a hard journey. It was challenging and downright scary. When passages were read about divorce, I wanted to die. In fact, a part of me did.

When I finally ventured out in all my "imperfection", I found a fellowship where no one knew me or anything about me.

My opening comment to the first woman I met was, "Hi. My name is Lori. My mother is dying, my daughter is suicidal, I'm about to get divorced, and I'm still mad at God."

I just dumped all my "Cindy secrets".

Nice huh? I figured if I was going to be judged, I might as well save her some time and put it all out there. But she never missed a beat. A pain-filled smile etched across her face, and she accepted the walking wounded woman before her.

God bless that woman. You're not going to believe what she did a few months later.

That little church taught expository style—they read and studied a book of the Bible verse by verse. Sometimes it took months before we would move on to a new book. Well, I had been away on a holiday with my girls for a few weeks and when I walked in the front door upon my return, there was my friend, anxiously waiting for me. She was such a Paisley. Wrapping her arms around me, she told me that we had reached chapter seven of 1 Corinthians . . . and she wanted to sit with me because she knew it would be a hard lesson for me to hear. (1 Corinthians 7 delves into marriage, divorce, and remarriage, and *is* hard for many Solos).

Ladies, that was love in action.

I was *still* struggling with God, with my mother dying, and with other dysfunctional stuff in my life. My journey with Jesus was very topsy-turvy and I was navigating with only one shoe—and at times, that shoe was pretty flimsy. It wouldn't have taken much to send me running away (or hopping, I guess), but this young mother was tuned in to my susceptible state. She knew the Word and realized what was coming. So she had flagged it in her heart and mind that when the pastor got to "that" chapter, she would walk with me through the hard, painful gravel pit of emotions. She would be ready to offer much-needed support to her limping sister. And it *was* hard, but she prepared me, prayed with me, and sat beside me. And our pastor, aware of my situation, was filled with grace, but stayed true to the Word.

I've never forgotten that morning.

A situation that could have crushed me and sent me reeling back into despair—running from the only One who could restore my soul—was instead defused by a sensitive, heart of gold. She sat beside me and held my hand.

She held my hand.

I'm convicted even as I write this (and also more than a little teary-eyed). Would I be aware of the needs of a sister who hadn't been attending very long? In the same circumstances, would I put myself out there for her? Would I?

Ladies, Solos are just like you and me. Whether they are divorced, widowed, never married, or attending alone because their husbands aren't church goers, they are all daughters of the King. I suspect many of them are exposed to more hurt than we can even imagine. Unless we have walked in someone else's shoes—their exact same shoes, not just fictional ones—we will never really understand their needs or what they are going through.

And what about wobbling two-soled-sisters? Well, truth be told, many sisters today are legally married, but emotionally divorced. My heart cries out for the brides who have a ring on their finger, but their heart in their stomach. They walk with two shoes, but at least one of them is broken and painful. Sadly, many of us are closeted Solos; we fake it and hide behind masks.

Under three things the earth trembles, and under four things it cannot bear up: under a servant who becomes king, under a fool who is stuffed with food, under an unloved woman who is married, and under a female servant who dispossesses her mistress. (Proverbs 30:21-23 NET)

My heart breaks for these sisters—those who are married, yet unloved. If this is your story, you need to cling to Christ, our Cobbler, as your all-in-all. Until you let The Cobbler get under the pain inflicted by the faux finish of your marriage, it's never going to get better. If your husband won't work on your relationship, then keep praying. Stay under the Master's hands, and find a trusted female friend, pastor, and/or spirit filled counselor to help you make the right decision.

And know this. No matter what your spouse says, you are beautiful.

You are special.

You are loved—fiercely and passionately—by the One who wrote love on His nail-scarred hands.

Yes, be careful what you wish for, Cindy. Some "happily" married women are, in fact, desperately lonely.

And for those Solos who are widows, I can't begin to imagine. My mom and dad are now with the Lord . . . but to lose my husband or children . . . that would be a heavy cross to bear. I pray you find healing and wholeness under the Cobbler's precious hands.

There's a woman I know who never married and remained single well into her senior years. I always wondered why. Then one day, I found out she had a secret that was shared with very few.

As a young woman in love, she had, in a moment of weakness, given in to her natural, sexual desires. Before the bed could even turn cold, he was gone, taking her precious gift of purity with him. She was devastated and embarrassed, seeing herself as someone "less than".

So she dedicated herself to the Lord and has led a wonderful, full life. But no matter how many decades passed, she kept limping in her soul. She had not forgiven herself for slipping. She didn't believe she fit in with the married women, nor did she feel that she could offer herself in marriage to any good Christian man. Her shame held her captive. She forgot the truth of the Great Exchange—of what Jesus did on the cross—and her true value and identity.

I spoke with another Cindy who said the worst wounds she ever received were from women in her church. She was divorced and felt like she was being kept at arm's length by every woman she attempted to get to know. She would try to engage people, but only found rejection. She concluded that married women were afraid she may steal their husbands.

Tired of feeling less-than, she tossed her Solo status, picked up a pair of running shoes, and made a dash for the door. She's never returned.

What a loss.

What a shame . . . shame on us for missing out on fantastic friendships because we feel insecure or awkward around a single gal.

Most churches do seem to be geared for couples and families, and I guess this is because programs and events are often planned to accommodate the masses. Cindy, that doesn't mean you are not wanted. However, the sad reality is that some of you feel

77

this way, and no doubt, many of you have been overlooked and misunderstood.

Here's a great comment from a Cindy Solo who has since found a mate:

"It does shock my friends and family members when I tell them I am still at the same church even though they have left me out of things many times. But I know that God has placed me in that church to help, to include other single parents that may walk through those church doors. Due to what I went through, I have since been working on a new class that our church will be offering. It is for step-families, but also for any single parent who wants to be married again, and in this way they will belong. I may have suffered greatly at the words and actions of other women in my church, but because of that, I try not to let other women go unnoticed in the church. One of the things that kept me in my church was knowing I wasn't there to win a popularity contest; I was there because I wanted a deeper relationship with God, I want to be the best Christian mom, wife, friend, daughter, sister that I can be, and I couldn't do that if I turned my back on God."

~34-year-old American

How about you?

Do you feel like a misplaced, mate-less sole?

Are you a Cindy Solo?

Please forgive us if we've ever made you feel awkward or out of place. Most of the time, it's without malice or awareness. We're all navigating our walk with Christ in footwear that don't always fit or function perfectly. In fact, no shoe ever does walk perfectly. We're all works in progress. I love what Ruth Graham chose for her epitaph on her gravestone, 'End of Construction— thank you for your patience'. Love it. We need to get this truth into our souls and apply this grace to ourselves and to other women.

Cindy, know this, there is absolutely nothing wrong with you.

The Cobbler does not see you as a hopper, but as His daughter—complete and designed for His purpose and plans. Singleness may be your calling for life . . . or maybe for a season.

Only He knows for sure. In the meantime, embrace your freedom and don't allow feeble feet around you to cause you to trip.

Cindy, you can wear Stilettos, Pumps, Loafers, Boots . . . the choices are endless! You are more functional than you know. Step out in faith, and ask the Lord to show you how to reach out and minister to others.

And if you've got some Cindy secrets buried deep, you know what I'm going to say? Yup, it's time to go sit on The Cobbler's bench and ask Him to examine you and bring your "stuff" into the light. Be willing and open to hear what He has to say, and respond when He reveals some dirt that needs to be cleaned up. There may be a label or two that needs to be removed (black smudges and all). Submit to Him and get fixed. Only He can remove all the things that are holding you captive. Rid yourself of all the enemy's niggling lies that try to tell you that you are "less-than" and "missing something".

You are complete in Him.

You are not forgotten.

He delights over you with singing.

Go dance in that truth—and with no midnight curfew!

As for us double-soled sisters, how should we relate to a Cindy Solo? For starters, we need to remember that we are all individuals; all of us are broken in one way or another. Each one of us need loving, non-judgmental relationships that see beyond our different sole issues. Our Cindy is a child of God. Her heart is precious, and we must reach out to her with warmth. Help Ms. Solo understand that her identity, just like ours, comes from Jesus—not from a mate, social status, finances, stuff . . . nor from her role in the church or world. It comes from Jesus, and Jesus alone.

In short, we need to accept her, cherish her, walk with her through whatever journey she is on, and encourage her to the use the gifts The Cobbler has given her.

And sometimes, we just may need to hold her hand.

7

Fiona Flip-Flop

Shoepidity: The act of wearing ridiculously uncomfortable shoes just because they look good!

If you came to my house today, you would see about five pairs of flip-flops at the front door and three pairs of "real" shoes. Okay, okay . . . eight pairs of flip-flops, by my hubby's count. So why all the flip-flops? Partly because it's summer, but also because my daughters and I, as do most women, like our toes to be free.

Maybe that's why so many people book holidays to warm destinations. There's something about removing ourselves from the busyness and responsibilities of life, and being spontaneous and loose for a bit.

Kind of like our friend, Fiona Flip-Flop. She's not a full-fledged member of the church, but she floats in every once and awhile . . .

Fiona pulled the stop request cord on the bus, signaling the driver to let her off at the next stop, right in front of her favorite park. As the rear doors swung open, she quickly finished her conversation with the teen girl who'd been sitting next to her on the short ride. "Here, take this," she said passing the girl a small green brochure.

"Jesus knows my name?" the young stranger read aloud.

"He sure does! The name of my church is on the back. It's that brown brick building, over there—across the street from the park. You should totally come sometime."

With that, the *swoosh* of the closing door ended their conversation. Fiona smiled and waved at her new friend's stunned face through the window as the bus pulled away.

Tilting her head back, Fiona looked up to the sky. "Thanks, Dad. That was sweet."

As if in agreement, the sun broke through the clouds, lighting up an area of grass in the middle of the park.

"Wow, I think I will join you for a bit!" Fiona looked across the street at the church, pausing for only a moment before making her way toward the sunny patch. Stretching out, she kicked off her sandals and opened her Bible to where she had left off reading earlier. Strains of *Amazing Grace* could be heard in the distance, and without warning, tears began to flow. *Oh how you love me, Jesus. I was such a wretch. So wicked. Thank you, Father, for your amazing grace.*

Laying back on the grass, Fiona clutched the open Word to her chest, eyes closed, in total abandon and worship of the One who loved her first and most. She could have penned the words of the hymn herself, and every time she heard it, something inside her broke. Not a bad kind of break, but the kind of break that rips down strongholds of the enemy, destroying every argument that goes against the truth of who she is now in Christ, and reminding her how much He loves her.

Yes. I once was lost, but now I'm found.

Yes. I was blind, but now I see.

Yes. Grace has relieved all my fears. Praise God! How precious grace is.

The Lord *has* promised good to her. Fiona studied His word intensely for years and was secure in her hope. Fearless, she is shielded and finds everything in Him. He is her all-in-all . . . through good times and tough times.

With the end of the song, Fiona felt the Spirit nudging her toward the fellowship building. Wiping away a few tears, she slid her feet into her flip-flops. Hauling herself off the dewy grass, she brushed twigs and straw off her long, yellow walking shorts.

Clouds had been pushed aside and the sun was out in all its glorious fullness. Rays bounced off the sharp pebbles that covered the parking lot, making them sparkle. She mused that the lot was like the yellow brick road, calling people into a place of refuge and peace. Before she got to the cement front steps, something caught her eye. She bent down, picking up a teeny, heart-shaped rock.

"Thanks, Dad," she said looking up, as she dropped the pebble into her pocket and headed inside.

The foyer was empty, save for an older couple that was being let into the sanctuary. The woman was in a wheelchair, and Fiona prayed silently. *Hey Dad, you know that woman's story. Make yourself real to her. Let her feel your presence. Heal her heart, soul, and body . . . show her your amazing grace.*

Fiona didn't rush into the sanctuary, but while still praying in the Spirit for the unknown couple, she stopped at the visitor's counter to grab a few more of Pastor Frank's little green brochures. She liked to keep a stash handy in the side pocket of her purse to give out. Jesus had changed her life, and she could not help but talk to anyone who would listen. The pamphlets were a great ice-breaker and gave the essence of the Good News.

Hearing another favorite song, Fiona slipped into the sanctuary through the side door, choosing the back row. She excused herself as she scooted her way in front of someone to an empty spot. Stumbling a bit, she lost her balance and stepped on the stranger's foot. *Sorry!* She mouthed.

The lady smiled and pointed to her protected toes. Boots! They both shared a discreet chuckle.

Pass Me Not, Oh Gentle Savior was now being sung, and once again, tears of gratitude began to pool. Smiling, Fiona joined in the chorus, not caring that she was a wee bit off key and looked like a wreck as rivers of tears made their way down her face.

Hear my humble cry . . . while on others Thou art calling, do not pass me by. Trusting only in thy merit, would I seek thy face. Lord, won't you heal my broken spirit. Save me by thy grace!

Fiona could sit still no longer. She stood, swaying and crying, hands raised in total abandon. She could not help but give praise and worship freely. Years before she had learned that in this conservative fellowship, she needed to hang near the back so as to not distract others in her moments of grateful freedom.

When the worship ended and the announcements started, Fiona felt as if she had been yanked from the very presence of God and flung into a boardroom. She struggled with the housekeeping part of churches . . . announcements, bulletins, programs and such. She flopped into her seat, opened her Bible and began to read.

It wasn't as though Fiona didn't recognize that a group this large needed some herding. She knew all too well about corralling people, but why not at the beginning of the service or via email? She also didn't feel called to be shackled to any programs or activities inside the church. Thus, whatever they were sharing during the announcements didn't matter to her. She had her own deal going on outside the walls of this building. She "did" church with a half a dozen women who "wouldn't be caught dead in an organized religion". Fiona smiled; she couldn't agree more.

Fiona's conversion—no transformation—occurred in a rather unconventional way. She didn't find Jesus at a church or an outreach. She found the Truth when she was paying back her debt to society during a six-year mandatory sentence at a maximum-security women's prison. Now she felt indebted to society! Her punishment turned out to be a gift; providing absolution from what would have been an eternal punishment. You see, it was during her involuntary stay that she observed a woman, Mandy, that seemed to command respect amongst the other inmates, yet had a softness at the same time. Very rare and not the norm when it came to "top dogs". It was Mandy who introduced Fiona to Jesus and discipled her for the last two years of her sentence. When Fiona's discharge day came, it was hard to say goodbye to Mandy—a lifer—but they promised each other to keep in contact. They have kept their monthly visits for over five years now. An amazing, true disciple, Mandy had flipped her hopeless situation into an amazing mission field, giving hope to many.

No, Fiona's faith was not about religion at all. It was about having a personal relationship with Jesus. It was a privilege to "be Mandy" now and help six unchurched women in their walk. Having signed away her life to Christ, Fiona lived to share His love at any cost. Seeing other women repent—with broken and contrite spirits—accept Christ and grow in the Lord was what she lived and died for. Much like Mandy, she was living out a life sentence that she gladly embraced!

The women met whenever their crazy schedules allowed, and the hours would pass like minutes. They would cling to each other, and almost always would laugh or cry at the end of each get-together. Fiona would tease them that they were all becoming like Ruth and Naomi. The story of Ruth from the Bible was one of her favorites as it so closely represented her own passion and love for gals down on their luck. Yes, Fiona and her unconventional worship group were working and walking out their faith together. It was so real—no masks, no pretenses, no games. Just real, like Mandy.

Fiona had tried once to bring a few of these new believers with her to church, but sadly, they were not warmly welcomed. In fact, one of them heard someone make a comment about their dirty feet. It took a whole lot of prayer and encouragement to help that baby sister get past the hurt.

Still, Fiona believed that one day, with a bit more growth and maturity—in the hearts of those within the church—her wounded friends would be welcome to join her.

But for now, she would continue to come when she could, soak up the praise and message, and leave. The teaching from Frank was always good and the notes she took were perfect to share with the others, opening up discussion. Each woman shared her ideas and questions in their little informal forum, and Pastor Frank and Brenda had been great whenever Fiona called seeking clarification on tough topics.

To Fiona, Sunday services allowed her another place to worship and learn . . . but doing church with Jesus and her friends was where real ministry occurred.

Oh, our Fiona! What a precious, free spirit she is.

Shall we examine these easy, breezy soles that flop into our fellowships now and then, or come frequently but aren't actively involved within the church itself?

A Flip-Flop makes a loud, distinct *snapping* entrance and exit. This girl is neither silent nor invisible. Fionas attend our fellowships when they can, taking resources and wandering around like they own the place. Fionas can generate more questions than answers—but wait . . . does she tithe here? Has she applied and been accepted into membership? Who exactly does she think she is?

Oh, that's just it. She *knows* who she is. She's a daughter of the King. You know . . . the One who bought the church with His own blood . . . who paid the penalty for all our sins—past, present and future.

As for her giving, that is between her and the Lord. She often gives more than ten percent of her income, but not necessarily to the bricks and mortar churches she visits. Fiona gives of herself at every opportunity in her community, and even beyond as she feels led. Somehow, on her journey with the Lord, she has not felt constrained to conform to any man-made structure or system.

Some accuse her of being lost in the seventies.

Of being a hippie Christian.

Or not being a devoted Christian.

It doesn't matter. Her sole is Teflon. No labels stick—old or new. The Lord alone is her judge. She has let go of her own life and sees herself simply as a Jesus lover.

And yes, Fiona Flip-Flop is often misunderstood and judged. She's not oblivious to what people say; she just doesn't care.

Let's hear from a few of these girls who don't seem to flipping care what others think:

> "I've always felt judged by women in the church and thought it to be a hypocritical place to be—something someone should NEVER feel in church. I've also felt that the church community as a whole is too involved in internal politics and run more like a business than a place of worship . . . I consider myself nondenominational and a child of Christ, not a doctrine."
> ~54-year-old Canadian

> "My problems with women stemmed from a need for a mother figure. All these mother types tended to dominate and control

me. I now look for sisters in the Lord. However, it isn't only women I have problems with. I have a creative, reflective type of personality that many cannot cope with. I just don't fit into the 'norm'."

~59-year-old Australian

"I mix in many Christian circles and LOVE the women. But when it comes to 'formal' church and 'formal' women's gathering, it's as if certain women are the judge and jury of what is correct and proper for the Christian reputation/appearance to stay unblemished. This leaves little room for transparency, authenticity, and vulnerability. I think our witness/reputation/appearance is often better served when we're striving less to be perfect and humbly accepting our weaknesses. I receive humor and humility better than judgment and legalism."

~47-year-old Australian

"I also know of women, in another local church, that got criticized by women for bringing the 'wrong brand' of biscuits for morning tea . . . and another Christian lady went up to one of my friends and offered to take her shopping to improve her wardrobe. We have nothing to do with this church body, well very little, as it seemed to us to be very toxic and discouraging. Very, very sad. Having said that, I have a couple of close Christian women friends, and we can chat and pray together as often as we need to—it blesses and encourages me greatly."

~27-year-old Australian

"In my homeland, church people knew me since I was a little girl. My family was overly involved in church, and although I wasn't leading or teaching, but simply attending church regularly, people respected me and my sometimes odd personality, and never put pressure on me to do anything."

~38-year-old Australian

"I don't affiliate myself with any denomination. I'm a Christian. While [visiting] a church, a woman behind me said to her husband, 'She's wearing pants.' I thought 'Wow! Are you kidding me?!' I figured that in some churches they're more legalistic about things like what a woman should wear at church, and just ignored the comment."

~52-year-old Canadian

"I have been a believer for over 30 years. I have been hurt, back-stabbed, ignored, judged and felt generally unloved by fellow believers. Through it I have been reminded by God that everyone has a story as to why they are the way they are, and they are at a different point in their journey with Him than I am. All I can do is love. Jesus commands us in John 13:34-35 to love one another as He loved. Nowhere does it say in the Bible to have expectations of other believers. God has taught me that when I am hurting I am to love that much more, and He is always faithful in revealing an important lesson to be learned in that hurt. It's usually to have a greater dependence on Him."

~No age or country given

It would appear that Fionas aren't totally unsusceptible to hurts, but typically, they are pretty resilient compared to other shoes. I would imagine it has something to do with flipping and flopping around without any hard surface protection. While that may seem contrary to what I'm saying, hear me out for a second.

When my daughter returned from a three-month mission trip, having been barefoot in flip-flops every day, the soles of her feet were black—like permanent ink. Even after a few hot, first-world-privilege showers, her feet were still hard and dark. It seemed nothing would permeate the thick skin. It took a professional with a foot bucket, scrubbing salts, and a pumice stick to soften them up. Without shoes, her feet had become hard for a good purpose—to protect her.

So it is with Fionas.

The Flip-Flops I know have typically gone through some harsh stuff. Their lives have taken them places and through things that most of us could not even imagine . . . or want to imagine. But the very experiences that toughened them up, have also made many of them extremely sensitive and caring to others.

Blessed be the God and Father of our Lord Jesus Christ, the Father of mercies and God of all comfort, who comforts us in all our affliction, so that we may be able to comfort those who are in any affliction, with the comfort with which we ourselves are comforted by God. For as we share abundantly in Christ's sufferings, so through Christ we share abundantly in comfort too.   (2 Corinthians 1:3-5)

I relate the Fionas of this world to the woman who came to Jesus and washed His feet with her tears, drying them with her hair. Jesus said, *"Therefore I tell you, her sins which are many, are forgiven—for she loved much. But he who is forgiven little, loves little."* (Luke 7:47)

Maybe this is what makes our Fionas so extreme—so "out of the box", or perhaps more appropriately, so not made for a box. I know every pair of flip-flops I ever bought were found hanging freely on a wall. You see, we—all of us—have lived lives under sin's death sentence, and were weighted down in lives void of purpose. But, when we meet Jesus and make Him Lord of our lives, when we are truly born again, we should have been radically transformed and set free. So we should love with recklessness. Love God. Love others.

Our Fionas really do get that. They live and love freely . . . and often with a bit more flare than most of us. They kind of go a bit wild, but wild in a good way. They express love in the same crazy way that He does—free and with abandon.

Francis Chan wrote a book, *Crazy Love,* which dissects the love of God and challenges us to rethink the gift of salvation. It is the gift that brings not only eternal life in heaven, but also a living, insanely intimate relationship with Him now—here on earth. If you're wondering about our liberated Fiona and how or why anyone would feel so compelled to weep and sway in worship, perhaps you may want to take a walk through Francis's book. Watch the short videos he made for each chapter as well. They were enlightening to me . . . and maybe for you too.

Now, if you're a footloose Fiona, and you've been flipping and flopping around a few church foyers, I hope you can use this chapter to help others understand you. If a frantic Betty Boot or Stella Stiletto asks you, yet again, to volunteer downstairs with the kids because "You don't do anything here", just give her a warm hug and word of encouragement. Let her know that you're a Flip-Flop, busy doing the Father's work elsewhere, but you will be praying for her.

That being said, I pray that you will also stay tuned into the Holy Spirit and be open if He calls you to shift into a different pair of footwear. Seasons come and seasons go. Some are short, and some are longer, but our feet and hearts need to be willing and ready to take on whatever the Lord calls us to do. We will only know that timing when we are obedient to the Holy Spirit's leading.

In the meantime, enjoy your freedom in Christ and, no matter what shoe you may find yourself wearing, never allow anything to constrict you in your wonderful expression of love and worship. You, Fiona, can teach us all how to walk freely! But, on that same note, Ms. Flip, don't judge other women who serve and adore the Lord in a more conservative way. The Cobbler searches and knows the heart of His gals, so we need to just relax and show respect to all.

Jesus came to bring life . . . and life more abundantly. Live, love, and serve accordingly.

As for we other soles who have our toes nicely tucked into a busy pair of more serious footwear, we may want to take a step back before we even think of judging Fionas. Yes, it can seem unfair that they live unencumbered while we are all stuffed into a structured shoe, but it's all about grace. His grace. He has given it freely to all. Who are we to try and press our earthly expectations onto these joy-filled gals?

Perhaps instead of judging, we should join them. We could have a special night where we all slide out of our normal footwear, put on some worship music and sit barefoot for a while . . . or even dance with the Fionas amongst us.

Before you hyperventilate over the idea of dancing before the Lord, remember David danced and he was called a man after God's own heart. If your breathing is still labored at the thought, then maybe just try it in the privacy of your own locked room.

Every Sole needs to open up and let loose her tight, cramped soul . . . to enjoy a few Mary minutes of worship in our busy and demanding Martha worlds.

Nancy Newbie

*It's not about the shoes. It's about what you do in
them. It's about being who you were born to be.*

~*Michael Jordan*

The most precious shoes I own are not really shoes at all, but
a pair of baby booties I wore many years ago. My mother had
stashed them away, and then gifted them to me when I became a
mother. Both of my girls wore them, and the booties are clearly
visible in each of our faded baby photos that hang above the stairs.
Those teeny shoes speak of innocence and the sweet, fleeting
months of babyhood.

Oh, how I love little baby soles!

Nancy Newbie flipped open her notes, closed her eyes, and
prayed that God would settle her rapidly beating heart. When the
pastor told Nancy he wanted her to share her testimony, she
thought he was a bit crazy. But week after week, he kept prodding
her. As nagging as his requests were, it was the constant,

unrelenting compulsion from the Holy Spirit that eventually broke her.

She finally agreed, and now here she sat, thinking of the irony of it all. She, a brand new Christian, speaking to a group that, for the most part, had been Christians all their adult lives. What she was being asked to share, if not anointed, would be rather hard to hear. Nancy waited, her head down, eyes closed . . . praying.

Having finished her Valentine's Day announcement, Stella returned to the seat beside Nancy. Opening her eyes, Nancy knew she was up next. For a brief moment, she eyed the fire alarm on the wall. It was only a few feet away . . . but as she was in the front row, she figured there wasn't much chance of getting away with it.

Pastor Frank was now at the podium, his eyes locked with hers. "This morning we are taking a very different turn. The Lord has been pressing on me to have the last Sunday of the month dedicated to hearing testimonies from some of our own. And to get things started, what better person than the newest attendee of our congregation. It's been interesting getting to know Nancy and watching her grow. The transparent, baby Christian questions she asks have impacted me, and my entire family. Let's all give her an encouraging welcome."

With that, applause broke out and Frank gestured her toward the front.

Nancy stood but her feet did not move.

She closed her eyes again, and begged the Holy Spirit to take over.

Suddenly, she felt a calm come over her as her heart rate steadied and her body fell into obedience to her brain. The stairs leading to the pulpit that had, two minutes ago, looked like the base of the Great Pyramid, were now mere pebbles. She glided up without thought. Frank had told her about the Holy Spirit's anointing, but this was the first time she'd ever felt His power.

Flattening out her notes on the sloped stand, Nancy smiled and began.

"Two years ago, my life was perfect. I had a great husband, a good job, healthy kids, a nice home . . . it was perfect, on the outside. But on the inside, I was miserable. Something was missing, and no matter how much money I made, or how many shoes I bought, I was unsatisfied. I know it's hard to believe that even shoes can't make us happy, but it's true!" She leaned in close. "Now before I go on, I need to say that I am not dissing shoes—I still have a slight obsession with them—but I recognize that shoes are just footwear. They don't change your life—no matter what Cinderella says.

"But back to my story. There was this woman, Marie, who would come into my office a few times a month. There was something different about her. She was the most confident, smiling woman I had ever met. It was rather annoying." Nancy let out a nervous giggle. "Marie didn't wear the newest fashions, or have an expensive hairstyle, but when she walked into the boardroom, she just . . . owned it. And it wasn't as if she had a fancy work title—she was our cleaner.

"You see, I was a bit of a workaholic. I would regularly stay after hours, and our paths would frequently cross. Marie would smile at me and say something nice or encouraging. Then she would just put in her ear buds, turn on her music, and hum as she emptied cans and wiped down the furniture and equipment. It drove me nuts. She had this . . . this presence of peace . . . that I couldn't take my eyes off.

"One night, it was just her and I. She put down her cleaning supplies and shared her secret. It was Jesus.

"At first I kind of cringed. It all sounded so cliché. But when she talked about Jesus, it wasn't about a church, or a bunch of rules. It was like she knew Him. Like, you know how when we go to a great movie or find an amazing shoe sale, we just have to tell our friends about it? That was how she was talking. Like . . . Jesus was real or something. And it wasn't like her life was a bed of roses; her husband had just lost his job and her daughter was a mess. But she had this peace . . . this amazing peace.

"I had gone to church when I was a teen, so I knew about Christianity and religion, but this was just not the same. I remembered "these" and "thous" and "shalls" and "shall nots". What this gal was talking about was nothing like I remembered. I found myself purposely working late on the days Marie would be in. We would just talk and talk. I was listening, watching, and asking, but I was not yet ready. Marie invited me to church, but I was too afraid to go.

"Then six months ago, I got a promotion and was transferred here to your town." Nervousness started to creep up on Nancy. She looked over her shoulder to Pastor Frank, and he nodded, as if to say, 'It's okay . . . keep going'.

Nancy took a deep breath. "My family was not at all happy about moving. So six weeks ago, my husband took the kids and moved back to our hometown. I was devastated, but too stubborn to give up my career. One night, I was overwhelmed with grief and anger—I was kind of losing it. One moment I would be crying out in anguish, and then the next moment I was fighting mad. So I pulled myself together and went to . . . the mall."

It seemed as if the whole congregation let out a guffaw. Nancy pulled out a tissue from her cardigan's pocket, wiped her nose and dabbed her eyes. "I know, right? Call it retail therapy. It was all I knew.

"Anyhow, I was in a change room when I found this little green brochure sitting on the bench." Nancy held up a tattered square of faded green paper. It was one of the church's *Jesus Knows Your Name* handouts. "I sat there in the change room and read the whole thing. For a second, I thought the cleaning lady from back home had written it. But, as you may know, it was written by Pastor Frank. So I called the number on the back—and I was still in the change room! Sorry if you were one of the women waiting for me to leave; I was in there for a long time.

"Well, Pastor Frank and his wife Brenda met me in the food court and, well . . . here I am!" Nancy shrugged her shoulders as if she was done, but Frank was shaking his head. This was not over. He wanted her to tell them . . . everything.

"Oh man. This is hard." Tears began to flow. "Well, I quit my job last week, and I'm moving back home to be with my family." The congregation broke into warm applause, but Nancy hushed them with her hand. "Pastor Frank and Brenda really want me to say something to you women in this church before I leave." Nancy could no longer look up. She was studying her pretty, pink baby Jane shoes. She looked back again at Pastor Frank, who nodded, then closed his eyes in prayer.

"Ladies, I've been attending here for a few weeks now, but I've been struggling for most of that time. You see . . . oh, this is tough . . . you see, most of you don't appear to have what Marie

93

had. Hardly any of you . . . shine . . . or seem to have that incredible warmth and love . . . or the presence of peace and gratitude for Christ that I saw in Marie. Not that I've spent a lot of time with you, or even met all of you, but just from watching you interact. You look so tense and cautious . . . almost afraid or angry at each other. I went to Brenda and we talked about it. She agreed that we're all missing out on something. Between our jobs, families, and busy church programs, so many of us are not living the kind of relationship-based fellowship that we should."

She looked back at the pastor, who was still praying. "That's probably why Pastor Frank sent me up here to talk about this—because if you get mad at me, I'm leaving anyhow."

Frank opened his eyes, smiled, and shook his head slowly.

Nancy continued. "It was something that I noticed, and I'm not saying this to be judgmental. It's just that if I hadn't had the seed of Truth planted in me by Marie, who was so in love with Jesus, I wouldn't have understood the message in the pamphlet. I'm still trying to piece everything together, and I don't really know much about . . . anything. But I do know that I want what that cleaning chick had. I want a living, breathing, real life in Christ. I want to know Him more, not just know more about Him. And, I want that for all of us. So, ladies, maybe it's time we get real—really real with Jesus and each other." She looked down again at her shiny new pink shoes, took a deep breath, and then looked at Brenda, who smiled encouragingly.

"To all you men, I'm sorry that I'm talking to the women this morning, but hey . . . this is my story so . . . it is what it is.

"Ladies, what if we were to stop judging each other, stop checking out each other's hair and shoes, and instead see each other through Christ's eyes? What if we were to lay down our lives for each other? I think in order to do that, it needs to start with me. And you. It's all about the lady in the mirror. We need to take off our masks. You know? The masks that have helped us cope through life by hiding behind them. But Jesus came to set us free!"

Nancy could feel her voice speeding up and getting louder, but she didn't care. "What if we were to love Him with full abandon, and walk with Him each day . . . learning to take on His grace for ourselves, and for others? Aren't you lonely like me? Aren't you tired? Don't you want a life that reaches beyond what's parked in our garages and hanging in our closets? Don't you want a relationship with Him, and with each other, that is exciting, authentic, and full of purpose?" Nancy felt herself break, and she knew her moment was over. This was what she had been called to share. It was up to the Holy Spirit and Pastor Frank to finish up.

As Nancy slid back into her seat, relieved that she was done, Stella's manicured hand reached out and grabbed hers. Nancy looked up and was shocked to see black, mascara-stained tears streaming down her face.

"Yes," Stella whispered between sobs, "I want that life too."

Oh, our new baby Christians! I just love their passion. They don't know anything from nothing and couldn't tell a Moses from a Matthias. Praise God! All they know is that Jesus loves them, died for them, and He wants a relationship with them.

It's actually sad that, as we educate and disciple these newbies, some of them get all tied up in knots and lose the excitement that comes from being newly born again.

Baby Booties aren't as common as other footwear (even though they shouldn't be that hard to find). Let's hear some thoughts on being new in Christ and in the church:

"Only been here a year, trying to find which one I am, want to be. A leader invited all the single ladies who work in a particular career stream to come to lunch. I was not invited. She tells me how wonderful I am (because of something I did once to help her) but she has never ever asked me anything about myself, so would not have known I fit the category. I am relatively new to the church and would have benefited from connecting with these women. I have learned to shut up since then, and I have really pushed into God to learn to show His grace to others. I have come a long way since the days of those offences and really focus now on God's will (for my life) not the acts of God (what I want Him to do)."

~No age or country given

"Christians give God a bad rap. It would be wonderful if people could just be real and honest. Let GOD be GOD. It sucks to be hurting and be judged. No wonder people go to programs. Tender hearts, unhealed hearts are being wounded in the name of people . . . it's not Jesus. Jesus came to heal and to set us free. People need to feel safe to heal. Let people grow from where they are at. Baby Christians are dying of spiritual crib death. Novice Christians go through hard trials and lack healthy coping skills, and have unhealthy life skills, and Christians give up on the 'unchurched, in love with Jesus' person who suffers loss and addictions and abandonment. Even call out judgments from the pulpit."

~No age or country given

Baby Christians dying of spiritual crib death . . . that's pretty graphic, huh? But it did get me to thinking about how careful we are when it comes to our own babies.

We have a new granddaughter, Hayley, and she is as tiny and precious as they get. I can cup her little feet in one hand and still have room to spare. Since Hayley isn't about to go on a hike quite yet, her footwear is mostly for her mom and grandmas to play dress up with. She's such a little doll.

You see, booties are not really shoes at all—just flimsy, knitted pockets to tuck baby toes into. They will help to keep them warm, but offer no true protection. It's up to us grown-ups to watch over our babies and keep them safe.

As newborns don't know how to talk, eat, or walk, they depend on us to help them in all aspects of their growth. Similarly, new followers of Christ need help, guidance, and to be spiritually fed. They are truly the most vulnerable soles in the church.

So, are you a Nancy Newbie? Do you stand in the back of the foyer, afraid to take a step or make a move in case you fall? Do you feel intimidated by these mature Christians—the ones who seem to have it all together, know all the songs, routines and scriptures? I sure hope you've had your eyes opened having taken a stroll in a few of our "grown-up shoes". We are all still learning . . . and falling . . . and sometimes tripping each other up.

Don't fret about your teeny feet; they will grow all in good time. Enjoy your season of new-birth and soak in His Word. See how Jesus walked and emulate Him because, let's face it, so many of us who walk among you are still getting parts of it wrong.

That being said, please forgive us for setting some bad examples of what a Christian walk is supposed to be. It's not that we want to cause you to stumble, but we are insecure in our own shoes and sometimes unsure of which way to go. Our own masks blind us from seeing clearly. So we step on each other, including you newbies. And yes, sometimes we just plain stomp. That's why The Cobbler's job is never done. He is constantly at work on each of us, cleansing, stripping, and refitting our soles to equip us to keep going and growing.

And to my grown-up sister-shoes, what a responsibility we have when it comes to our Nancy Newbies. They are watching us. They are looking to see if what they know is what we show. Ouch! In three out of the four gospels, Jesus warns us,

"Whosoever causes one of these little ones who believe in me to sin, it would be better for him if a great millstone were hung around his neck, and he were thrown into the sea."
(Mark 9:42 – see also Matthew 18:6, Luke 17:2)

Call me crazy, but I think Jesus is rather protective of His baby-shoed women.

I think we all need to take a careful step back—in whatever shoes we're wearing—and think about how we are walking out our lives. Are we merely churchgoers? Or church doers? Are we humble servants to any and all, or only to a select few? Are we talkers and tellers, instead of listeners and encouragers? We're called *to be* the church, not go to one. We're called to live and breathe in Him. His Spirit, His very essence, should be a fragrance on us that draws others to Him.

I'm afraid some of us have this wrong. Instead of being filled afresh, like Nancy Newbie or Fiona Flip-Flop, we are still walking in our dead old selves, stuffing our soles with odor eating inserts in an attempt to hide the truth.

Ew. That's just a nasty and yucky thought. I can almost see rotting skin cells bunching up in the toes of our shoes. Yes, no matter what style of shoe we are, there's no one who couldn't benefit by taking a stroll to the good ole Cobbler's shop. Frequently.

Better that a sole is cleansed by His healing, cleansing flow, than to offend and be tossed into the sea, to drift and eventually sink.

We need to run to Jesus. He is our hope. Our joy. Our peace.

Sally Sprinter

Forget the glass slippers, this princess wears running shoes!

The only time you're ever going to see me run—by choice—is if I'm chasing an ice cream truck. Yes, I do have a few good pairs of running shoes stashed away in my garage. I used to love playing tennis; someday, I'll pick up my racket again. Until then, I have tucked the laces under the tongue and stored them in a cabinet . . . just in case. (You never know when you may hear a beckoning ice cream truck song.)

But, there *are* many women who actually choose to run, and not because they're desperate for a decadent frozen caramel bar. They do it for . . . I'm not too sure why. The commercial said, 'Just do it,' but never clarified. I presume for fun.

Sadly, others lace up to run away, as I did, from Christian fellowship. I even attempted to outrun God. (Hint to any of you considering this—He runs faster.)

As this is the last shoe we're going to try on, let's switch it up a bit and hear first from a few runners . . . and a couple who are, in my opinion, in danger of bolting . . .

"An entry for this would be hard to come up with, as things just tend to 'snowball' with me. It is like a bunch of little wounds just stick to an enormous ball of misery somewhere inside, which started long ago and to which I've been adding over the length of my life."

~58-year-old, no country given

"I have a relationship with Christ but I cannot stand the relationships in church anymore. They have become so fake. It is so sad to see and experience."

~35-year-old American

"Women in both our last churches were total control freaks, power hungry, play their games, and they would only let you volunteer in the area they wanted you in—not your gifting. I always had a struggle with any new church my husband and I attended. I would be judged because I was pretty or smaller/slimmer . . . They would not like me because of who they THOUGHT I was and mostly that began with my looks and how they viewed themselves . . . I was always friendly, outgoing, and confident. In the end pride got in the way, one woman started a rumor, gossip spread and we left the church."

~44-year-old Canadian

"I don't expect the church to be my doctor, financial expert, or parents, but a kind heart is more helpful than a cold shoulder. I have only been able to find a few genuine female friends at church. I am very protective of my past. I have been abused and don't trust people well. I have found the women in the church are not approachable unless you are in their group. I have noticed if you are a working mom you are not 'in' the right group."

~No age or country given

"Too many churchwomen feel the need to project perfection when they feel so flawed inside. They sometimes realize they are phonies and then feel worse."

~55-year-old Canadian

"Here's my biggest concern—instead of embracing people who think or act differently, I have found Christian women to be quick to judge. My guess is this is because they mistakenly feel a different point of view is a judgment of their own beliefs. Here is a classic—the full-time working mother. When my children were young, I wanted nothing more than to stay home, but finances didn't allow it. I had women tell me I wasn't being a good mother because I was 'pawning' my children off during the day. My heart was already breaking; trust me, I didn't need to feel any more condemnation!"

~50-plus Canadian

"I moved away from a very loving church family. In my new town I have attended two churches. One for three years and the new one for almost two. We have lived here almost five years. I have reached out, invited women for coffee to my home, started a ladies Christian book club, started a bible study (no one showed up for either, which I kept open for five weeks with multiple announcements; each group was spaced two years apart), invited couples for dinner, attended two different small groups, attended women's studies, served in women's ministries. I do NOT have one single friend here. NOT ONE. I was friends with almost every woman in my prior church. NOT ONE friend here. I hurt deeply all the time over this."

~40-plus American

"I opened up to a several women who were involved in the same volunteer work as myself. It was a bad move. I thought we were developing rapport and moving to a more intimate relationship. Instead I was excluded from social activities. Not sure if this was because I am single or appeared to be wounded or weak. It was a crappy experience and was the final straw that made me leave the church."

~60-plus Canadian

101

Sally Sprinter bent over her feet and pulled hard on the laces, double knotting them. It was Sunday—her favorite running day. The rest of the week her runs were always cut short due to family responsibilities. But Sundays were different; they were her days to go for it. She could run as far and as fast, or as slow, as she chose.

Checking out a few different routes on her GPS, Sally chose one she hadn't done before. It cut through Millennial Park and then along the river. It sounded like just what she needed.

"No, Bella, you're not coming with me today, girl," Sally tussled the long, floppy ears of her Great Pyrenees. "This run is for me—Mommy time."

Disappointed, the mutt took a longing look at the leash hanging on the wall and collapsed onto the floor in obedience, rolling over to expose her belly for at least a good rub.

"Ah, Bella. You're such a good dog."

Sally slipped a second water bottle into her belt, put in her earbuds, and headed out the door. Her latest playlist filled her heart and mind with energizing tunes as she bounded down the road toward the park.

Years ago, she would never have been found running—especially on a Sunday. There was a time when Sundays were reserved for church and heavy, roast beef dinners. But after a brush with breast cancer three years ago, Sally decided to volunteer for a local fund-raising walk. It was there she met a bunch of ladies who encouraged her to take control of her recovery and health. Each night, long brisk walks helped her to sort out the chaos in her head. Soon, she and some of the other volunteer women started a running group, *"Up-n-At-M"*. Sally relished the strength and power she was finding within herself.

It was only a few months into this new healthy lifestyle when Sally's friend Julie was diagnosed with stage three breast cancer. Sally visited at first, but being so soon after her own brush with the miserable disease, Sally couldn't handle seeing Julie so frail. It was a scary reminder of her own mortality. So, instead, she chose to organize a 10K run fundraiser for Julie—that she could do!

Being the lead of the volunteer group, however, meant having to give up some of the duties she held in her small church.

Her resignation was met with much resentment from a few. Bitter, judgmental words sent Sally into a tailspin. One woman even made mention of all the meals they had provided for her family when she had been sick. Sally couldn't believe it. Clearly there were expectations attached to the "acts of service" . . . and Sally was not meeting them.

Where did this come from? How could they say the things they did? She was already grappling with *Why God? How could you allow me to get cancer? And then my dear friend?* The coldness she felt from "His people" drove her further away.

In contrast, the ladies from her running group rallied around her event. The fundraiser was a big success, Julie recovered and the rewards of running-for-a-cause became a strong attraction to her. In fact, as time went by, she felt repulsed by the closed-minded people from her old church. More often than not, Sally found herself skipping services in favor of a good run. Eventually, her attendance fell to Christmas and Easter . . . it wasn't as if she was missing anything. As her life got busier, her Bible slowly got pushed aside and buried beneath magazines, clutter and shoes.

Sally rounded the corner and turned into the far south-east corner of the park. The path took her by the playground and out toward the open fields, where a border of cedar trees made for a lovely shaded run. *This may be the perfect route for my next event.* It broke her heart to hear that Julie was sick again, but it only solidified her resolve to help. Ms. Sprinter was in the middle of organizing another fundraising run in her honor.

She continued along, following the prompts, jogging on the spot while waiting for a safe time to cross the road and head to the river. The GPS was guiding her toward a narrow easement that ran parallel to a church parking lot, but it was fenced off and no longer accessible. Without missing a beat, Sally worked her way across the gravel lot, running next to the blocked path.

Suddenly something sharp dug into the inside of Sally's heel. Hopping to a full stop, she bent over and dug into her shoe with one finger. Out popped a sharp piece of gravel. Then another. *What the heck?* She had laced up tight . . . how did they get in? Taking another step, Sally felt a third annoying pebble. As she bent over to pull off the compromised shoe, she saw something familiar; parked by the side door of the church was her friend Cindy's distinctive convertible.

Cindy was part of *"Up-n-At-M"* and had invited Sally to try her church, but Sally saw no need. In fact, Cindy had once given her a cheesy, green brochure. Sally was polite and dropped it into her bag, but misplaced it before she could read it.

Laughter and cheers from inside the church could be heard over her playlist. Sally pulled out the earbuds. Laughter? In church? And now clapping? She turned off her music and tried to hear what was going on.

Intrigued, Sally put her shoe back on, laced it up, and walked toward the building. Gingerly she opened the glass door that was right in front of Cindy's car, and peeked inside the foyer. A young man was just about to close the dark, sanctuary doors, but not before Sally caught a glimpse of a woman about her own age standing at the podium. A woman preacher? Maybe this church was different.

The young man kept the door ajar and motioned for Sally to enter in.

Still curious, Sally agreed, but she didn't take a seat, choosing instead to stand in the shadows against the back wall. It would appear that she hadn't missed anything yet. The woman was just starting . . . and she was no preacher. That was for sure. In fact, she was kind of rambling, but there was something about this gal.

Sally listened, but mostly she watched. She couldn't take her eyes off the speaker, who was kind of lit up from inside. She wasn't overly eloquent or well-spoken, but she was enthusiastic . . . real . . . raw . . . and, it would appear, a bit shoe obsessed.

Wait. What? Did she just say she found a green brochure? Hey— could that be the little booklet Cindy gave me? Sally let out a small laugh. *Would be too funny if it was the one I lost! What a coincidence that would be.*

Whoa . . . this girl has got guts! Leaving or not, she is totally calling out the women in this church for being fakes. Good for her! You go girl!

From her vantage point, Sally could see quite a few women in the side sections. Heads dropped, tears fell. One woman started to sob, her chest heaving. Tissues were being pulled out of purses all over the place. What was happening here?

The speaker returned to a seat in the front, and a man in a suit took the podium.

"Nancy, thanks so much for sharing both your story and the burden the Lord placed on your heart for our women here. You are going to be sorely missed, young lady." The man smiled and appeared to be speaking directly to her, as if she were the only one in the room. There was something genuine about this guy.

"Now, I truly believe God wanted the women of our fellowship to hear this message, and to take it to heart," the pastor looked around, "but I believe He also wanted the men to hear it. We men need to love, respect and support our wives . . . and the other women here as well. It's true, so many are struggling with busy lives full of adversities and secrets. Sitcoms have made it the norm to mock and tease our spouses and the opposite sex. It's got to stop. The women in our fellowship need us to respect, encourage and come alongside them."

Clearing his throat, he continued, "When Nancy reached out to Brenda and me, it was only natural for us to invite her to plug into our church and be discipled amongst us. But . . . Brenda? I'm sorry, hon, but would you please join me up here?"

A middle-aged woman edged out of her seat from the center near the front and made her way up to the podium.

"Brenda didn't know I was going to do this—neither did I—but, sweetheart, would you please share from your perspective what we've been working on?"

Blushing, the obviously shy woman stepped up to the pulpit. She pulled down on the microphone, took a few deep breaths, smiled at Nancy, and then looked across the sanctuary, slowly from one side to the other. "Well, let me tell you. When Nancy came to us after a few weeks of attending our church and asked us why we didn't seem to be "real" like the woman who had witnessed to her back home, Frank and I were a bit . . . put off." She smiled. "It's never easy to be called out on something—especially when you've poured yourself out day after day, year after year in ministry. I mean, my first reaction was . . ." She looked down at Nancy again. "My knee-jerk reaction was to tell you to mind your own business!"

Nervous laughter spattered throughout the congregation.

"But, thankfully, the Lord bridled my tongue and I just sat and listened. We poured tea, talked, then cried, prayed, and cried some more . . . and then I told Nancy that what she was saying was resonating with me. Frank agreed, but we weren't sure what to do with it all. So Frank and I went home and prayed, and then began to really look at the New Testament church. We fasted. We prayed some more. And we cried . . . a lot. It was so hard to think about the hours and effort we had invested into the lives of you all, only to realize that we got so busy being . . . busy . . . that we all lost sight of what the true calling is.

"To make disciples.

"To follow and obey Christ, and in doing so, bring others along—like Nancy. To live lives that are so exciting, Spirit-filled, and powerful that others want what we have."

Brenda stopped and looked back at her husband. He came and stood with her. "Ladies," he said softly, "I'm so sorry. We are both so sorry for shepherding you in a way that led you to lives full of busyness, but with inadequate emphasis, first and foremost, on having an authentic, intimate relationship with Christ . . . and with each other. Like Nancy said, God wants us to live radical, free lives that are full of Him.

"So, before we close with a song, please know I truly believe the Lord wants us to start something here today. He knows you need each other in your walk with Him. We're going to stop being program-driven and rethink our mission statement. We're going to reach out to each other and build relationships not only here at church, but also in each other's homes, in coffee shops, in parks." Frank's eyes lit on Cindy with her leg extended into the aisle. "And even while running or playing volleyball." Cindy smiled, and Frank continued. "It's great to share the gospel, but to what end if we aren't living it out in our own lives? We need to be Spirit led—not led by my dictates. If you're tired of living independently from Jesus and each other . . . if you're ready to get real amongst your sisters—and that means accepting each other without judgment or spreading gossip—then would you prayerfully make your way down front so that Brenda and I can minister to you?"

Pastor Frank paused as women started to shift in their pews. He motioned to the praise and worship team, cueing them to begin.

Brenda took back the mic, her words were quiet and loving. "This standing together is not to be taken lightly. It's a public confession to other women that you are committing to bare your soul, to take off your mask, to be real, and to truly love. I want that to be my way of life; I want to be a light. Come join me."

The praise and worship team started to play.

Softly and Tenderly Jesus is calling . . .
Calling for you and for me.
See on the portal He's waiting and watching.
Watching for you and for me.
Come home! Come home!
You who are weary . . . come home . . .

Sally leaned back against the wall, wishing it would swallow her up. She watched as women all across the sanctuary rose and made their way to the front. On her right, a mousy woman reached across the aisle to a crying woman in a wheelchair. With a nod, she wheeled her up to the altar.

At the front of the room, Sally noticed a super-tall, make-up smeared, Amazon woman, clinging and sobbing against the woman who had started this whole mess.

Then she saw Cindy, hobbling on crutches with her bandaged foot, making her way to the front, where she dropped to her knees on the stairs in front of the podium.

That's Cindy. Oh, wow. I love that girl. The pull on Sally was growing, causing her to press even harder against the wall. Closing her eyes, she tried to hold back, but her feet could not stand still. She began to gently jog in place, only a few fingers making contact with the wall. *Jesus, help me. Forgive me.* With the silent prayer barely finished, the tentacle of unforgiveness and resentment that was tightly wound around her heart toward Christian women—and God—began to loosen. As she stood praying, bitter, dead roots were ripped from their anchored spots. The last, stubborn root that held her captive—anger—lost its hold . . . and hope began to spring up in its place.

Who am I kidding? My life isn't perfect. It's . . . empty. I miss growing in the Word and sharing tidbits over coffee with fellow believers. But I can't go up front. I can't . . . no way . . . but . . . A dam broke deep within Sally, sending tears cascading. *Jesus help me!*

Warmth filled her heart, and she stepped away from the wall.

And she ran.

Without regard to how she looked or what people would think, Sally ran toward the group of women who were ministering and loving on each other. And back to the One who loved her first and most . . . and had been pursuing her no matter how fast or how far she ran.

It would prove to be a run like no other—life changing. A race that she was determined to run well, and no longer alone.

Ladies, if we're going to run, it's best if we run into The Cobbler's arms. Oh how He is waiting for His lost, running sheep to come home. Jesus said:

> *"What man of you, having a hundred sheep, if he has lost one of them, does not leave the ninety-nine in the open country, and go after the one that is lost, until he finds it? And when he has found it, he lays it on his shoulders, rejoicing. And when he comes home, he calls together his friends and his neighbors, saying to them, 'Rejoice with me, for I have found my sheep that was lost.' Just so, I tell you, there will be more joy in heaven over one sinner who repents than over ninety-nine righteous persons who need no repentance."* (Luke 15:4-7)

I love how there is rejoicing and joy in heaven when one . . . the lost one . . . returns.

Let's examine an athletic shoe, shall we? Truly, they are an important shoe to have. They give great arch support, absorb the shock of a hard pavement walk, and when laced up properly, give excellent ankle protection. Any cardiologist would tell you running shoes are a key to a strong heart. It's dangerous to live a sedentary life as a couch potato. No, we are designed for movement and running shoes help to keep us healthy (maybe not so much if we're chasing ice cream vendors). That being said, the direction and destination we choose needs to be considered carefully. *The heart of man plans his way, but the LORD establishes his steps.* (Proverbs 16:9)

The Cobbler is so good! He doesn't want Sally Sprinters to give up running . . . but He desires them to run to Him, and with Him, not away from Him! He wants everyone to use their own unique design and testimony to share Jesus with others. We aren't called to be *of* the world, but we are called to be *in* it. Go out and be a light!

If you're a Sally, how about encouraging your running group to meet in homes each month to learn and study God's Word before a run? Teamed with the Cobbler, you can be changing lives, running after the things of God as you accumulate miles on your fitness tracker. (I'm not against fitness. I watch and read about it on a regular basis.)

But seriously, if you're a Sally and you've run from fellowship, or perhaps you're just lacing up getting ready to bolt due to messed up shoes stepping on you, would you please forgive us stumbling sisters? Can I encourage you to recall some of the other shoes we've examined? Not that there's ever an excuse to act in a way that is contrary to how the Lord has called us to live, but the reality is we just don't know where other soles have been, or where they are now on their journey. They could have attended church for fifty years, but be still struggling in baby shoes, having not been properly fed or equipped.

Or maybe they just grew out of their baby booties, but are not yet grounded in the Word. In their passion for Jesus, they come off as pointy, opinionated or pushy.

Perhaps their feet are so busy leading or working behind the scenes that they don't even realize they've stepped on your toes or offended you.

And maybe, just maybe, they have been so hurt themselves . . . so taken advantage of . . . so fearful of allowing anyone to get close to them . . . so . . . broken that they need the Cobbler every bit as much as you do.

Oh, how we need our Cobbler—our Savior!

Mercy. We are all a bit tipsy and sometimes unstable in our shoes, aren't we?

Thank God for His love and grace!

To all of you who have been hurt by one of God's flawed women (or men), I am truly sorry. I am sure there have been many times that I was busy serving the Lord (or just chatting in the foyer) and passed someone by. I know there have been times, when in my introverted, tired existence, I have ignored others, or appeared to look right through people.

God, forgive me, and I pray you will as well.

Indulge me a moment while I share a story.

My sister-in-law and her children were once in a serious car accident. The financial and physical ramifications greatly affected her family. Doctors, medications, and constant pain filled her days and months.

But here's the thing.

Not once since the accident has my sister-in-law blamed Toyota. But shouldn't she? After all, it was a Toyota Corolla that hit her.

No, that would be silly, wouldn't it? Yes, Toyota was the creator of the vehicle, but it was human error that caused the harm. That would be like throwing out a brand new, gorgeous pair of Louboutins because you tripped getting out of the car. That would be senseless and wasteful. And totally not advisable . . . (but if you insist and they're a size seven-and-a-half, send them my way.)

All that being said, before you toss out your relationship with The Cobbler due to some insensitive footwear in His church, take a moment and realize that He is not to blame for hurts inflicted on you by others. Don't be angry at The Cobbler for what His shoes do. It's slightly crazy that He chooses to be represented by sinful humans, but that's the deal. And humans mess up. A lot.

God loves you—fiercely—and it pains me to hear that so many of you have turned away from Him, or refuse to open yourself up to any Christian fellowship due to old wounds and horrendous experiences. I'm not trying to play down anything that's happened to you. Many of you have suffered straight out abuse at the hands of "God's people" but there are some amazing women out there who do love the Lord and want to get to know and love you.

To all you Running Shoes, give us—and God—a chance . . . will you?

If you haven't already, take a moment to kneel right where you are and yield to The Cobbler. He died for you and wants to give you an exciting, love-filled life. Not just an insurance plan to avoid hell, but a personal relationship with Him here on earth. You would have noticed in every shoe's story, that there has been a connection to a little green brochure, *Jesus Knows Your Name*. I've included a copy for you at the back of this book. Take a read and then please email me and share *your* story.

Finally, let's finish up this jaunt with a quote from a runner who read the above car accident analogy of mine some years ago:

"I understand God wasn't driving the Toyota, but man, does He need to give some driving lessons to those people He allows in the driver's seat."

~50-plus Canadian

Section II

Fit Is Everything

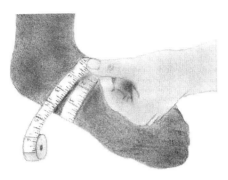

Taking Measurements

*Don't try to squeeze your toes into shoes you've
outgrown . . . Let them go so you have room for
a shiny new pair!*

~Jane Lee Logan

If you're scratching your head thinking, '*I don't know which
shoe I am . . . I think I'm a few of them*' . . . well, you're not alone. Most
women will identify with several styles because there are shoes for
every season. I'm not talking spring, summer, fall and winter, but
the seasons of our lives. Life seasons can be years, weeks, days or
hours. When looking at my own life, studying the survey responses
and interviewing other women, it became very clear that we switch
shoes often. This is a good thing because some shoes are just not
fun to wear.

All around the world, women are hurting from their
interaction with various "soles" met on the path of life. And a few
aren't too thrilled with the pair they're currently wearing either.
They'd love to exchange their shoe for a more stylish or

comfortable fit. Almost everyone surveyed communicated their desire to find healing, restoration, acceptance and authenticity.

So who were these women that responded to the survey? And what do the numbers say?

I Almost 83% of respondents regularly attend a place of worship. This isn't surprising, as the survey was gathered through a Christian women's website.

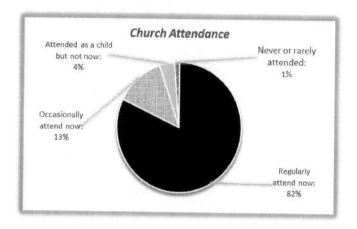

II When it comes to our interaction with each other in church, we are unstable on our feet as we struggle to establish true friendships and fellowship with a sad 11% feeling as though they never fit in.

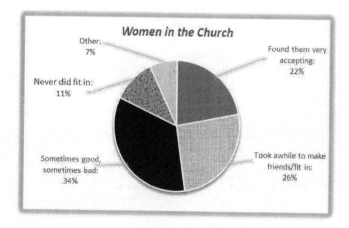

III   Being authentic is rare. When it comes to getting real, over half admitted to only letting a few women see their true selves, but even then, most kept a careful distance.

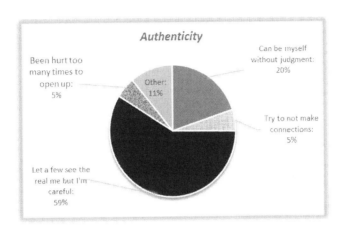

IV   Although there were a number of issues cited by the respondents, there were two main ones. The majority of women in the church were perceived as:

        i.   Creating cliques and putting up walls to keep others away

       ii.   Too busy sizing up the ladies around them

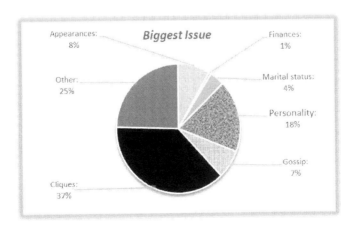

Disturbing responses, huh? But let's not panic just yet. All is not lost, and church life for women is not doomed to permanent dysfunction. These numbers represent feelings, not facts. Our perceptions and assumptions can be deceiving. Like the time I grabbed a perfect pair of pumps off a sales rack. The shoebox showed they were size eight, but as I struggled to force my foot in, it became obvious they were a size smaller placed in the wrong box.

In the same way, as we heard from our stories, we often place people into boxes to which they don't belong. Or we find ourselves somewhere we don't fit. Is it any wonder we often end up feeling disillusioned, discouraged and dismayed? Not to worry. Yes, the survey has shown us where we are failing and not measuring up. But there is hope. Sometimes we just need a good cleaning and an adjustment or two.

11

The Right Fit Makes All The Difference

One shoe can change your life!

~ Cinderella

My mother Joy loved the story of Cinderella. As a result, my daughters and nieces were well versed and slightly over-exposed to the tale. She made all her little princesses dress-up outfits that included plastic "glass" slippers and, of course, much coveted tiaras. They would prance and dance, pointing their toes out from beneath their long gowns to be sure they were seen by all. At tender preschool ages, they had learned the power of the shoe.

And the right fit.

What a different turn the little cinder girl's life would have taken if her ankles were swollen that fateful fitting day. Monthly water retention, or a twisted ankle from slipping on a freshly washed floor, could have brought devastating consequences.

As the story goes, dozens of women from the village tried in vain to get Cinderella's shoe to fit, only to find that it was not a one size fits all. That shoe was not meant for anyone but Cinderella. Glass slippers, after all, are unforgiving and not designed to stretch. Which makes me wonder . . . what about us? Are we forgiving? Are we willing to stretch? Do we accept other women just as they are—scuffs, muddy toes, broken heels and all—or do limit our contact to a select few?

From what I've personally experienced, and from what others have shared, more often than not we don't allow others much wriggle room. Instead of reaching out, more than likely we pull and tug at our sisters in an effort to fix them. Instead of seeing them as people to simply love, we too often see them as projects in need of our help.

I wonder if the Lord cringes at the sight of us grabbing bare, tender tootsies and shoving them into shoes they were not designed for. Do our words and actions cause Him as much pain as we are inflicting on these poor souls?

I dare say yes.

We may be good shoe shoppers for ourselves, but I believe we are often poorly equipped when it comes to assessing our sisters-in-Christ. We have an epidemic of women being pigeonholed into poor-fitting roles within the church, all because they were pressured to volunteer for jobs the Lord has not called them to.

But sometimes we get into footwear predicaments all by ourselves.

Remember when the shoe style of the day meant stomping around in those six-inch platforms? They were all the rage. I giggled at the first few women I saw wearing them. Alas, I soon fell victim to the fashion phenomenon, and found myself teetering on the edge of destruction as my shaky forty-something feet tried to navigate stairs. Yes, sometimes we embrace the most ridiculous things, not giving proper thought to what is sensible, but just wanting to fit in.

We all have several different styles of footwear in our closets, under our beds, and piled at the front door. There are the fancy going-out-on-the-town high-heels, the running errands flats, the flip-flops for the beach, and the sturdy boots to get yard work done. Necessity and common sense dictate that we adjust and change to suit the seasons and purposes of our days.

So it is with our spiritual lives.

In my fifty-plus years on this planet, I have worn, and lived, every shoe we have met on our journey. The most painful, but fastest growth period I went through was when I wore running shoes. Alone in my room with my Bible, a half-dozen devotionals, and my Strong's Concordance, I worked out my salvation and applied The Word—the balm of Gilead—to many open sores and a few hard bunions.

A year or so later, I knew it was time to reach out and trust women again. Walking without fellowship can be dangerous, particularly if we're left alone for too long.

Two are better than one, because they have a good reward for their toil. For if they fall, one will lift up his fellow. But woe to him who is alone when he falls and has not another to lift him up! Again, if two lie together, they keep warm, but how can one keep warm alone? And though a man might prevail against one who is alone, two will withstand him—a threefold cord is not quickly broken.

(Ecclesiastes 4:9-12)

We are designed to be together. Not necessarily all of us in massive sanctuaries, but absolutely spending regular Jesus time with one or more of our fellow believers . . . however that may look.

So how are we supposed to treat each other?

Older women likewise are to be reverent in behavior, not slanderers or slaves to much wine. They are to teach what is good, and so train the young women to love their husbands and children, to be self-controlled, pure, working at home, kind, and submissive to their own husbands, that the word of God may not be reviled.

(Titus 2:3-5)

Clearly, Titus 2 is not in practice in a lot of our fellowship circles. If so, my survey would have been dead in the water. No, for whatever reason, many churches—like many of us individually—have rejected the pattern set by The Cobbler and strayed way off course.

We are not measuring up.

"My husband is a Pastor, and I have seen a lot of this. There are a lot of contributing factors I believe to this issue. One of which is the fact women are often times working and very busy. We are so busy that all we have time to focus on is our to-do list, our agenda ... We are so narrow-sighted that we don't think about others. Secondly, I believe that Titus 2:3 is not being followed. The older women are not taking under wing young ladies and teaching them what they should be. The older ladies are not to be 'false accusers'. This is exactly what gossip entails and a lot of it is in our churches."

~ 32-year-old American Pump

But here's the thing—we're all human. We're all struggling to walk with confidence—without stumbling or stepping on toes. Some of us are not only wearing uncomfortable shoes, but we are also being smothered by masks. We go to church and, in dealing with our own unique pain, find ourselves snapping at someone, joining in a gossip circle, or hiding in the bathroom crying. We are afraid to be seen as we truly are because we've seen and heard horrible things that have happened to those who made themselves vulnerable and shared. As a result, for our protection, we use whatever coping skills we're comfortable with, such as blending in and doing whatever the rest of our group does, squatting in the last row of pews, or as a last-ditch effort at self-preservation, we never even leave our homes.

This is not what we were commanded to do!

Like it or not, we were not designed to be an island. We are not meant to play life safe. Best-selling author, Francis Chan, has a short video on YouTube called 'Balance Beam'. This video sums up in four minutes how we typically try to operate and live, contrasted to how God wants us to walk. So many of us put walls of protection around ourselves and our families, only to ultimately discover we have missed out on a life of meaningful interaction, purposeful vision, and powerful interventions.

And let us consider how to stir up one another to love and good works,
not neglecting to meet together, as is the habit of some, but encouraging
one another, and all the more as you see the Day drawing near.
(Hebrews 10:24-25)

Do we stir up one another? Sure we do! But sometimes our stirring up resembles the stirring up of a wasps' nest rather than encouraging another's soul and spirit. Whether intentional or not, we say and do things that cause the buzzing to start, and it gets louder and louder until the roar overtakes the fellowship and His house is blown apart. And everyone gets stung.

Do we encourage one another? Well, I've heard from many women who have been encouraged, but not always in a positive way. Consider this lady from down under:

"I felt judged, and quite frankly, looking back I see how that's exactly the outcome they wanted. They didn't want fringe people. If we were not prepared to get involved, we should really just leave."
~38-year-old Australian Running Shoe

This is not the kind of encouragement that we should be giving . . . encouraging others to leave. No one should feel they have to work to be part of the body. Several women—most of them Loafers—were asked to leave their fellowships because their introverted personalities were misunderstood. What a shame for the body to lose these precious, soft souls.

Some will be quick to remind us that *"All Scripture is breathed out by God and profitable for teaching, for reproof, for correction, and for training in righteousness, that the man of God may be competent, equipped for every good work."* (2 Timothy 3:16-17). This being God's Word, shouldn't we correct our sisters? Of course we should, but there are appropriate times, places and approaches. When offering correction, it's vital that we are so full of the Holy Spirit that our words call the other to repentance, leaving them feeling competent and better equipped—not crushed.

Iron sharpens iron, and one man sharpens another. (Proverbs 27:17)

Ain't that the truth! Yet, this verse is often quoted in order to justify harsh attacks on a sister. At times, we *will* accidentally rub each other the wrong way, which is understandable given our sinful human nature. However, when we do see the need to correct each other, we should be gentle, like a fine-gauge file, lightly buffing out a rough edge . . . not a metal mallet banging and flattening someone on an anvil. Too often, we get this wrong.

The Cobbler designed us to fit together and complement each other—a unique shoe closet of women of all ages, from diverse backgrounds, in all stages of repair (and disrepair), in different seasons, and with different sole styles.

For by the grace given to me I say to everyone among you not to think of himself more highly than he ought to think, but to think with sober judgment, each according to the measure of faith that God has assigned. For as in one body we have many members, and the members do not all have the same function, so we, though many, are one body in Christ, and individually members one of another.

(Romans 12:3-5)

With all the drama and pain we inflict on ourselves and others, I've heard from many women who have laced up their running shoes and made a permanent dash out of the church. Their sensitive toes grew tired of being stepped on again and again. Alone, they found solace with the Lord in their homes, where He became truly their All-in-All. Sadder still, are those who have turned their backs on The Cobbler all-together due to words and actions from His shoes.

Before we start looking around to see if any of our sisters have an issue that needs fixin', we need to first take a good look in the mirror. We need to understand who we are in Christ, and recognize our own issues, before we think of pointing out the flaws and failings we think we see in others.

"Judge not, that you be not judged. For with the judgment you pronounce you will be judged, and with the measure you use it will be measured to you. Why do you see the speck that is in your brother's eye, but do not notice the log that is in your own eye? Or how can you say to your brother, 'Let me take the speck out of your eye,' when there is the log

in your own eye? You hypocrite, first take the log out of your own eye,
and then you will see clearly to take the speck out of your brother's eye."
(Matthew 7:1-5)

Once we've come to grips with the size, shape, and purpose of His design for our lives—even if just for a season—then, and only then, can we progress to **live out** and **love out** the way He has called us to. Like little Cinderella's shoe, it's important for us to remember that women are not created to be one size fits all. We each need to find our place to fit in, while still being true to who we are and where we are on our journey.

Ladies, we are never going to get this down perfect. We need to do our best, but in the end, please know this—The Cobbler's love conquers all and never disappoints, even though his shoes sometimes do.

12

Are You in the Right Shoe Store?

Strong women wear their pain like stilettos.
No matter how much it hurts, all you see is the
beauty of it.

When my niece was getting married, I remember how excited I was to need a new pair of shoes in order to properly celebrate her upcoming nuptials. As it wasn't going to be an outside wedding, I knew I could safely purchase a lovely high heel without fear of sinking into a grassy chapel.

My daughters and I headed out to shop—first to Cabela's, and then to the Running Store.

Say what?

Now that would be ridiculous, wouldn't it? To shop in a sporting goods store for a formal pair of stilettos. Yet, from the survey responses and conversations I've had with women, it appears many shoes are strolling into the wrong "stores".

126

Several introverts are attending massive mega churches, and are popping Ativan to manage the crowd, or slipping in late and leaving early to avoid the crushing pressure on their soft, quiet souls. They think this is okay:

> "We arrive and leave quietly, hoping no one will prevent us from doing so ..."
> ~38-year-old Australian Penny Loafer

This is not God's design—that we would feel it necessary to sneak in and out of our place of fellowship. Don't get me wrong. I've so "been that shoe, done that"! But remember, we are created for some interaction, to be with others for encouragement, and to build up one another in faith.

We shouldn't run.

By far, most of the running shoes I have spoken with are introverts. However, they are not the only ones struggling to find the right place of worship. I've also known Spirit filled, amazingly gifted, extroverted teachers and worship leaders who have felt stuck and underutilized in a church that did not need their gifts. At first it may be refreshing to have a break and a sabbatical, but before long, your soul will ache to let God's gifts flow.

Now, this doesn't mean that you dust off your sandals and move on to a new fellowship. No, first pray and ask the Lord if He has something different for you right where you are. There may be a need that The Cobbler wants you to fill, but He hasn't revealed it to you. Maybe it's just not time yet, or perhaps it is not an official ministry within the church but something completely "out of the box".

As a teacher, I remember walking through this dilemma when I attended a very established church in a small town. They didn't know me from Eve, and even if they did, all the classrooms were occupied by diligent and capable Sunday school leaders. A few idle months later, I had the "weird" idea to start a women's book club. We would read a Christian fiction book and meet monthly at a nearby restaurant for fellowship and discussion. The first month there were eight of us. Six months later we had grown to sixty women—including quite a few unbelievers who wanted to be a part of our close-knit and fun group. Had I hunkered down and sulked that my church didn't need me, I would have stifled God's gifts in me, and we would never have experienced this wonderful club.

Sometimes you just need to think outside of the shoebox.

If you're a worship leader but the team is already full, what about opening up your home to give voice, piano or guitar lessons to the next generation? (Preferably, whenever possible, as a time offering—without fee. One never knows the talent that sits undeveloped due to tight family budgets.)

If you're an introvert or housebound sister, perhaps prayer is the answer. Some of the most amazing prayer warriors I have ever met are the quiet women who are typically viewed as "on the sidelines" Christians. How wrong we can be! Or how about starting a texting prayer chain? Or use social media to encourage and uplift others? How about one-on-one visitation? Ask the Lord to press on your heart a woman who is lonely or hurting. It may be a neighbor, or the mail-lady, or even one of your caregivers. Open up your home and life to others.

And whoever gives one of these little ones even a cup of cold water because he is a disciple; truly, I say to you, he will by no means lose his reward.
(Matthew 10:42)

It doesn't need to necessarily be cold water.

Years ago, I was desperately lonely after having moved into a new subdivision. I assumed I wasn't the only stay-at-home mom feeling this way, so decided to put out an invitation to a few neighbors. Let me tell you, I was full of insecurities, but loneliness trumped fear. As my neighbors arrived, we realized we all had toddlers, and soon the living room was full. Emerging from the kitchen, I was the last to join the small crowd. The awkward silence and sudden hush made me wonder what I had missed. Tea cups were balanced on knees and every eye in the room was on me. As I leaned forward to pour my own brew from the pot on the coffee table, I was mortified to see a layer of dust rise and swirl to the top. I looked around at knowing faces. A few pretended to take a sip of their tainted tea, but when I burst out laughing, they all joined in.

Wonderful friendships were formed that day over my blunder. Decades later and many miles apart, those friendships continue via Facebook. Laughter will do that. Things don't have to be perfect. You just need to step out and be a friend.

Moving to a city years later, the Lord brought a few women across my path that confessed to knowing the Lord, yet did not attend a "real" church. This was a new thing for me. I loved these women, but for years I could not wrap my brain around their choice. I am embarrassed to admit that, at times, I would feel a little condemnation rise up in me regarding their choice to walk alone. Can a shoe be a shoe if not found in a box?

Yes!

As I joined in fellowship with these women, it became very apparent that they were deep in the Word and prayer. And I mean *deep*. They would never turn down coffee dates or any chance to meet together in twos or threes. As our friendship and trust developed, they shared various reasons as to why a Sunday, bricks and mortar church did not work for them: shift work, not finding a comfortable fit, being introverted, being stepped on and still limping . . .

The thing is, they were not upset or freaking out about their experiences. They were more than comfortable in their sole condition and had peace. Their growth in Christ was staggering. They loved people, cherished the Word, and shared their faith. There really wasn't anything dysfunctional about them; although they, like all of us, would benefit from some adjustments by the Cobbler's skilled hands.

"For where two or three are gathered in my name, there am I among them."

(Matthew 18:20)

In their own small group, these women had found a place to worship, grow, and fellowship that fit.

Now, let me tell you, when I shared this with a few pastors, I was chastised. I was told that by not being under proper authority, these women were in danger. One pastor even believed these women needed deliverance in order to be set free.

I mulled that for a bit, spoke with the different women, and I prayed.

Sigh.

In a broad sense, they may need to be set free, but then again, don't we all? We will work on that when we go to the Cobbler's shop. We'll also examine the different shoes for different seasons, but for now . . . can we just agree that maybe, just maybe, we can be a healthy Christian without signing a denominational membership card? Again I say yes.

Some shoes are meant to be kept in boxes. Others do better in the open air, hanging freely. God loves them all!

I am in no way calling for an exodus from traditional churches, but as the days on this earth are being wrapped up, I see more and more gatherings of believers that don't come with a tax-free status number. As a result, these gatherings have more freedom to teach and live the whole Word of God.

My husband and I still love our fellowship, but we also "do church" regularly with others . . . everywhere! Attending church doesn't have to be a "this or that" thing, and it's not just because we *need* to meet together often—we should *want* to!

Now, as to the style of worship and the size of the congregation, truly we need to be where we feel led and where we fit.

There is nothing more daunting than trying to find a new home to worship. Often people say that they "just knew" they were home when they walked in the door.

But what if you've walked through dozens of doors and still feel homeless? Or worse than that, after weeks of futile searching for common life forms, you begin to feel like an alien?

That's kind of like a year ago when hubby and I felt led to leave our wonderful, mid-sized church. Many of our friends questioned our decision. I mean, we loved the denomination and were quick to push and "sell" it to others. We respected and loved our pastor, and we had some really good friends there, too. But we knew the Lord was prodding us on. To where, we had no idea.

One Saturday night, as we sat on the couch wondering how we had got it so wrong, I had the impulse to google "House Church". Up near the top was a listing for a fellowship that met in a nearby home.

We clicked on the website link, reviewed their statement of faith and found it was solid. We listened to a portion of a sermon, and then stared at each other.

Seriously? What would our friends think? How could the Lord use us in a teeny, tiny place like that?

We opened our minds and hearts, and went the next morning. We've been attending that teeny, tiny church for over a year now, and it is home. It's unlike anything I've ever experienced or thought was "right", but God is so present there too. The size of a congregation is not indicative of the Holy Spirit's presence.

I wondered if this approach was too radical. I mean, what about the formal church board and yearly annual meetings, or the structured programs and newsletters? But then I realized, aren't casual, informal gatherings the way Christians walk-out their faith today in communist or persecuted countries?

Isn't this what some of the churches looked like in the New Testament?

The churches of Asia send you greetings. Aquila and Prisca, together with the church in their house, send you hearty greetings in the Lord.
(1 Corinthians 16:19)

It's something to think about.

So, just because a particular "shop" isn't right for your style of shoe, don't trash it or forbid anyone to enter. It may be exactly where they are meant to be.

As a kid, I was raised in a celebrated denomination with very strong viewpoints. By the time I was a tween, I was of the opinion that if you didn't follow the exact doctrine that we did, you were deceived and would, sadly, be lost for eternity. "Narrow was the way", and that was how I interpreted our doctrinal beliefs and style of worship.

When I reached High School, the Lord brought an amazing diversity of fellow believers into my path. I was awed by the fruit in their lives, and as we spoke and shared, it became apparent that I had some things wrong. These peers who I had believed were lost, were actually teaching me how to walk with Jesus, and how to study and apply the Word. They led me to new depths of truth. We, Baptists, Pentecostals, and Missionary

Alliance young people found encouraging, healthy fellowship together. We found unity around the cross and on common key salvation doctrines. Beyond that, sometimes we joyfully agreed to disagree, but we didn't allow ourselves to get caught up on any minor differences.

Who would have believed that was possible? Certainly not me before high school.

As I grew and matured, I again came across many more people who held slightly different doctrinal views, but who all loved the Lord fiercely. I learned that I could actually worship and study in various churches. As a Berean, I would test the teaching of course, but no longer did I feel stuck in a certain denomination.

Sometimes dissimilar thoughts and styles of worship can bring damage to souls when—in zealous defense of our preferences—we spout off and demean the choices of others. I'm not talking about the necessary exposing of false, salvation-stealing teachings, but rather, trivial things like whether or not to have drums.

"I dread carrying on a conversation because they are so extremely opinionated about everything—a young family's difficult children, a girl's purple–streaked hair, a song during worship that they don't care for, the fact that the drums were used during the traditional service, the horror that the worship pastor wore a 'dressy hat' to lead worship."
~43-year-old American Pump

Sometimes discussions like that happen amongst our own fellowship. We can't even agree with those who agree! One woman told me years ago that her church split over choosing the color for the church nursery. I kid you not! How did we ever get things so very wrong?

Now, if you're a running shoe, don't close the book in disgust, convinced that you were right all along. These behaviors of churches and church women are not okay. Nor is it how God designed us to interact. In Acts, we read how there was a person teaching wrong doctrine, but others approached him in Christian love:

Now a Jew named Apollos, a native of Alexandria, came to Ephesus. He was an eloquent man, competent in the Scriptures. He had been instructed in the way of the Lord. And being fervent in spirit, he spoke and taught accurately the things concerning Jesus, though he knew only the baptism of John. He began to speak boldly in the synagogue, but when Priscilla and Aquila heard him, they took him aside and explained to him the way of God more accurately.

(Acts 18:24-26)

Thank God, Priscilla and Aquila didn't drive him out as a heretic:

And when he wished to cross to Achaia, the brothers encouraged him and wrote to the disciples to welcome him. When he arrived, he greatly helped those who through grace had believed, for he powerfully refuted the Jews in public, showing by the Scriptures that the Christ was Jesus.

(Acts 18:27-28)

The Lord used Apollos—this imperfect person who was a bit off theologically—to greatly help, powerfully refute, and lead people to the Lord. Yes, thankfully Priscilla and Aquila treaded softly and discretely to correct and direct him. Following the gentle correction, Apollos was still accepted by other believers and encouraged to stay in ministry. There's a very important lesson in this chapter, which is why, no doubt, the Lord included it for our benefit.

Yet, there are times when it's just best for us to agree to disagree. While some function well in mega churches, others are best found in small congregations, quiet home gatherings . . . or even in coffee shops. Much like the shoes they hold, boxes are not all one-size-fits-all.

We need to find the right fit for us, and not judge those who worship in a different kind of way.

Because you shouldn't be looking for a pair of stilettos in Cabelas.

Section III

The Cobbler's Shop

13

A Thorough Examination

*A lie can travel half way around the world
while the truth is putting on its shoes.*

~Mark Twain

Years ago, when I was "perfect", I would listen to other women's struggles and prayer requests, tilt my head and judge them to hell and back. Abortions, sexual sins, wayward children . . . Clearly they were not walking a true Christian walk.

Right?

I grew up in church and was rather smug in my status—a virgin bride, outstanding mother of two obedient children, and an active servant for the Lord. Yep, I had the whole Christianity thing nailed down. Anyone with a messy life was to be pitied, prayed for, and most importantly, kept at arm's length. After all, I couldn't have their dirt contaminate my clean life. (Of course I never shared with anyone any of my secrets; I sure knew how to fake it.)

Ah, the superior life as a female Pharisee!

Years later, separated from my husband and with a divorce looming, many church ladies reached out . . . to condemn and doom me to hell. I was reeling. Weeks and months later, most apologized, but the damage was done. Lacing up my running shoes, I left the fellowship of believers as fast as I could run. In my race to get away, I also left God behind. I wanted nothing to do with anything or anyone that would add more afflictions to an already deeply wounded woman.

But God.

He pursued me and wooed me. After a few months, I started to slowly begin to trust the One who loved me first and most. In awe of His holiness, I became keenly aware of how unholy I was . . . and had always been.

But what about church? Could I dare walk into one? As you know, I did find a safe place to heal, and an amazing Paisley Pump to walk beside me.

Watching this precious sister's love in action made me realize that I was never a perfect Christian after all.

Neither was she.

None of us are. Nor can we expect to be.

My journey of healing, restoration, and understanding Christ's grace, has been interesting. Confession, repentance, and getting real before God and my fellow sisters has been a crazy, beautiful experience. The Word became not a weapon of mass destruction to fling at others, but a source of healing for my soul. I realized I had spent decades walking various church foyers full of arrogance. My aloofness and haughty spirit must have wounded many. I'm so sorry.

After a few months of gentle restoration, I sought His will and new direction. I believed my hypocritical life—especially the damage I incurred during my "running years"—would deem me unusable. Nevertheless, I laid out my life before Him and waited to see what He would choose.

To my surprise, He chose me—not in spite of my sinful past, but because of it.

My eyes and heart were opened to women around me. I was released to love and embrace without judgment. The first group God led me to were sexually exploited women. Women like the one at the well. Women like me.

From there, He led me to dozens of ladies who had left Christian fellowship. Women who laced up and ran away after being wounded by "perfect" church people, never realizing that those same people were just as damaged in their own way. Women with a common message of rejection, hurt and isolation.

The reality is we're all broken. We're all wounded. We all inflict wounds. That's the consequence of living in a fallen world. But just like when taking measurements we start with ourselves, God showed me restoration and reconnection starts with each individual too.

We need to step down from our haughty places and take a good look at ourselves. Regardless of our testimony, we all need a Savior. There is no hierarchy of sin or of sanctification. When we measure ourselves against His Holiness, we find the truth. His holy throne is *the* leveling field. Oh, how we need Him, and each other.

Church itself is not the answer. Jesus is. But as we've already learned, walking without fellowship can mess us up.

Chances are, if we are teetering up on our holiness ladder—faking it, living as female Pharisees—we are eventually going to fall. We best climb down and get real with ourselves and with Him . . . and the sooner the better. Only then can we make authentic connections with women in every situation. Much better to stand secure, side-by-side, than alone aloft.

The Word says the lost will know we are Christians by our love, but do they know?

In order to be a witness and reach the lost, we need to work on the problems and relationships within our fellowships. Each of us need to address our own wounds, find healing, and then be brave enough to put ourselves out there and get real. Together, as we sit side-by-side at The Cobbler's feet, we will learn how to accept each other's soul conditions and extend love.

So how's your shoe?

Is it tippy? Hard soled? Seriously soiled? Or scuffed and marred from being stepped on again and again?

The point is that our "stuff" always seems worse than the other gals'. We have an accuser, and he loves to shine the spotlight onto our insecurities and stir us up. Lies and labels that have followed us—some of them from childhood—tell us again and again that we are not worthy. Or that we are not useable or loved; that we are discount rejects and belong in the goodwill box.

But what is true?

The thing the devil never wants us to fully grasp is how valuable we are and how much we *are* loved.

It's time to own the truth. Say the following verses out loud (if you're in a coffee shop, just mouth the words—people will just assume you're a slow reader).

Pay careful attention to yourselves and to all the flock, in which the Holy Spirit has made you overseers, to care for the church of God, which he obtained with his own blood.

(Acts 20:28)

Knowing that you were ransomed from the futile ways inherited from your forefathers, not with perishable things such as silver or gold, but with the precious blood of Christ, like that of a lamb without blemish or spot.

(1 Peter 1:18-19)

The Lord your God in your midst, The Mighty One, will save; He will rejoice over you with gladness, He will quiet you with His love, He will rejoice over you with singing.

(Zephaniah 3:17 NKJV)

Wow. The Creator of the universe . . . rejoices . . . over me . . . over you . . . with gladness! If you are lonely—or have never felt truly loved—this verse is for you. Soak in it.

He sings over us. How romantic is that? My man loves me, but I would die if he sang over me. The man is tone deaf. But if you've heard the birds of the air sing, the tinkling of a brook, or the wind rustling through the trees, you've heard the symphony of God's love. He designed harmony.

Does that not fill your heart with courage to know that He is so into us? He is the Lover of our souls.

While He loves our souls, we women love soles! And, along with that, shopping for them. Let's imagine for a moment that we walk into a store, pick up a pair, and slowly turn them around and around, examining and admiring the shoes from every angle. We flip them over and look at the price tag—on sale for fifty dollars!

Pulling off the shoes we wore into the store (in utter disgust—what were we thinking when we bought them?), we toss them to the side and try on the shiny new pair. Standing in front of the awkward floor-height mirror, we imagine how our lives would change if only we had them. Now we're getting committed.

Leaning next to the rack, still staring at them with wonder, we begin to mentally go through our wardrobe, considering what outfits would complement the coveted heels. Nothing? No worries. In fact, all the better, now we can shop some more!

We slip them off with much care, placing them gingerly in the proper box, and walk to the till. Opening our wallet, we count out fifty dollars in bills, having carefully considered the shoes' value. We pay the cashier what we have decided is a reasonable price for the beauties, and an exchange is made—an equal and fair swap.

Now, here's the thing. The Creator of the whole universe looked at you. He examined and considered you—just as you are with all your sin and faults—and He said, "I love her. I want to spend eternity with her."

Remember, Zephaniah says that He delights in you and sings over you, (I've delighted over shoes but never sang over any). Well, the Cobbler does sing, and He took out His heavenly wallet and paid for you, not with a twenty, not with a fifty, but with the precious blood of His Son.

Stilettos, Pumps, Running Shoes, Baby Booties, Loafers, Flip-flops, Boots, Singles, and Misfits—He loves us all.

Girlfriend, you are priceless. No matter what anyone has said to you or about you, please recognize your value as a daughter of the King, and the great exchange that was done on your behalf. How precious are we who are redeemed with such a costly currency! Now there's something to dance about . . . I think I just may need a new pair of party shoes!

14

SOAP and Stretch

If Cinderella's shoe fit perfectly . . . Why did it fall off?

Have you ever bought a pair of shoes where the price tag has left an annoying, gummy residue on the inside? Or even worse, the price was written in permanent ink on the bottom and is viewable when you walk? (Yes, I shop consignment—don't judge.)

I remember once getting a prestigious pair of pumps at a goodwill store, but upon bringing them home, could not get rid of the sticky, square mark on the inside. Whenever I wore them, my pantyhose would adhere to the spot, and cling when I took them off. (It was like stepping on gum on the sidewalk—only *in* your shoe. Can you picture it?)

This was not a problem when I was returning straight home, as I would just pull until it would snap and release. However, when I was going to a friend's for coffee, it was a different matter.

As this was years before the Internet and search engines, I was left on my own to figure out how to rid the gorgeous leather pumps of their one annoying flaw. Glancing through my pantry, I pulled out a box of cornstarch and dumped it on the spot. Taking my thumbnail, I pushed the powder-covered goo from one end of the shoe's inner lining to the other. It worked to get rid of the sticky factor, but now the impressive name brand was smeared black and barely readable—and I was kind of proud that I had a pair of "those".

So I went and got my nail polish remover.

A few rubs and the offensive black smear was gone—as was the trendy, fashionable label.

Seriously?

Was it so bad that I wanted to have one snobby, obviously expensive pair of shoes—even if they had been gently used, perhaps by a Stella? I had actually looked forward to leaving the name exposed when we all left our footwear at the front door during the next ladies' group. I'm almost embarrassed to admit this, but that was where my heart was at. Crazy, huh?

It took a while, but thankfully the Lord took care of that prideful attitude. No doubt, He who sits in the heavens laughs—a lot.

However, there have been a few labels I've borne that were no laughing matter. Names that brought shame.

How I struggled to remove those labels. Sexually abused as a child, there were lies and names that went back as early as I could remember. Talk about a stubborn stick—I had worn them my whole life. Later, with blurred sexual boundaries, my teens left me vulnerable, and therefore, one of "those girls". A bit loose but not "undone". More labels. Still years later, when I got divorced, I imagined a big red "d" stuck on my forehead.

And even now, almost daily, the accuser keeps flinging a few new hurtful lies my way. Sometimes they stick for a bit, other times they fall right to my feet.

What's a girl to do?

'Therefore, if anyone cleanses himself from what is dishonorable, he will be a vessel for honorable use, set apart as holy, useful to the master of the house, ready for every good work.'

(2 Timothy 2:21)

We need to be cleansed from not just the things that have been stuck on us by others, but also our own willful junk. Like anything that needs to be washed, **SOAP** is the obvious place to start.

I learned this acronym a few years ago from a lovely, forever friend, and it works wonderfully. It will remove those nasty, sticky labels without goo or damaging your manicured nails. It's a daily discipline that is crucial to keep our souls clean.

The first and most important step, and one that should never be missed, begins with the letter **"S"**.

SCRIPTURE

We need to actually open up the Bible and read it. I saw this with some of the women who didn't regularly attend worship, but were really into the Word. I guess since they were not being fed on Sunday mornings, personal time in Scripture was survival for their souls.

In contrast, I have quite a few church friends, who never miss a weekly church meeting, but rarely open their Bibles on their own. I know I've gone through seasons like that, and oh, the dirt that collects in our lives as a result!

Some people's devotional times look like they stepped off the page of Pinterest. They are Instagram worthy. Often women will post pictures of their quiet times on social media. I'm not totally against this, as long as their hearts are with the Lord, and they are not just looking for "likes" from others. *But when you pray, go into your room and shut the door and pray to your father who is in secret. And your Father who sees in secret will reward you.* (Matthew 6:6)

I remember when I was a stay-at-home mom, I had a lovely ritual of morning tea, with my Bible propped on the big, stuffed arm of my favorite chair. I would curl up and devour the Word before the girls woke.

Years later, I tried to maintain that habit, but didn't succeed. I had a job that required me to be at my desk by 7:30 AM. My mornings didn't begin with the Lord, and resulted in me walking out the door with my soul in a terrible condition.

Recognizing my need for Jesus time, and my desire to give Him my first fruits, I realized I needed to tweak my morning devotions in order to actually do them. They are certainly no longer

Instagram worthy—who would want to see a dark picture of a mascara–smeared pillow, wet dots of drool still visible? You see, now I lie in bed and pray, asking God to reveal Himself and His Truth. Then, still under the covers and in the dark, I read His Word on my smart phone. (Probably the only wise task I do on the silly, distracting thing.)

God says His Word will not return void (Isaiah 55:11) so I figure a nibble of His Bread in the dark is better than nothing. Sheila Walsh recently published a book, *5 Minutes with Jesus,* as she too realized that many of us are missing out. Proverbs 31 Ministries created a free app called, *First 5,* with the same reasoning. So often, we think if we can't give Jesus an hour, we'll just skip our devotions all together. The girls from Proverbs 31 are brilliant as *First 5* is designed to set your morning alarm through the app which in turn hijacks your cell when it goes off. You can't connect with social media, email, voicemail or anything until you first connect with The Cobbler. I love that it encourages us to give God our first fruits of the day.

Thankfully, there are days when I do have a bit more than five minutes. I drag my tired bones to the couch, pushing the button on the coffee maker as I go by. On the ottoman is a small journal, and this is where I write out the **"O"** part of SOAP.

OBSERVATIONS

I'd like to say that every day I pull some serious, deep observations off the pages . . . but that would be a lie. Some days, my eyes and heart are on autopilot and reading the Word is just going through the motions. This is not the ideal—but it's true. (Remember girls, we're being honest with each other now.)

The mornings when I am more coherent and less rushed, I love to jot down a few observations that pop out and resonate. Weekends are typically deeper, as I have more time and am usually more relaxed. But here are a few quotes from one of my "tired" mornings, just to show that we aren't always talking huge truths, but little morsels.

- John 4
  - Woman at the Well
  - Disciples confused but learning not to ask dumb questions

- Father who believed in faith in contrast to the "Lord I believe, help my unbelief dad" (I was comparing the father in John 4 to the father in Mark 9:24)

Those are my notes without edits. Not really earthshattering or anything crazy wonderful, but these were the thoughts that tweaked my heart that morning. In simple, quick, observational notes. And yes, this was a workday.

Jesus said that we need to not just hear His Word but do it (Luke 8:21), so the next step in SOAP, **"A"**, is important as well.

APPLICATION

So I've taken in some scripture, and made a few observations, now what? To close the Book (or the app) and walk away without going deeper would be totally short-sighted. And unwise. Before I move on, I stop and examine myself to see what is convicting and moving me.

Let's see what my notebook revealed under my **A**:
- Who am I? The believing dad or the struggling in faith dad?
- A less than perfect woman whom the Lord can use to bring others to Him

That morning I jotted down both a question and an answer. It's not about filling out a page in a journal, but rather taking away something that will fill a void or crack in your life. And to remind yourself that no matter what your state, the Lord can still use you.

And now, as things are exposed and out in the open, we need The Cobbler to finish the cleaning, using the final letter, **"P"**.

PRAYER

Whether you write it down or just speak to the Lord, daily confession and repentance is key. As great as it is to learn and reflect, we need to ask Him to finish the work.

Once you've taken down some "O's" and a few "A's", read them over and approach the throne. Remember that you are going before a Holy, Almighty God. Confess where you have fallen short, stumbled, or flat out rebelled. He already knows, but He wants *us* to acknowledge our sins and "feel sick about them" (have a contrite spirit). When it comes to prayer, He's not concerned about fancy words, but rather about the truth we are speaking.

Much like how sincerity may be in question when a child who is caught chewing an ill-gotten cookie, says sorry while smiling from ear to ear, our heart and true intentions are known to the Father. To repent means to change one's mind and to desire God's way. I think sometimes if we were honest with ourselves, we'd have to admit that there are moments when we are spraying cookie crumbs as we are praying.

Ask for forgiveness with a sincere heart, knowing only He can wash us clean. We want the labels and lies from the accuser to be lifted and cleansed from our lives—fully—because there's nothing worse than gum stuck to the bottom of your shoe (except maybe when it's stuck to the inside of your sole).

Whew. I feel better already.

But what if our soles are still tight and a bit unforgiving? My word, is there anything more painful than ill-fitting shoes?

Not to worry—there are at least five ways to get those unforgiving shoes to loosen up.

STRETCHING

I The Painful Way
First of all, there's the old-age method of just wearing a pair of shoes as is—trying to force change. I'm sure we've all done this, ladies. I know I have. I slide on a pair of my hubby's thick work socks, and then force my bulky feet into the offending footwear. With winces and whimpers, I stomp around our house for a few hours, praying that the pain will stop and transformation will come.

This rarely works.

II Applying Heat
Failing the stomping around the house method, one might turn up the heat instead. You'll still need some oversized, thick socks, but instead of walking it out, grab a blow dryer and set some time aside to make those shoes hot. There is no movement on your part this time. Just hunker down in a comfy seat, turn on the appliance, and point the heat wherever you find offense. It feels kind of good and

productive to blast something, but be careful not to give your tender toes more heat than they can handle.

This technique does change a shoe, for sure, but it also poses some safety issues. It's been said real leather footwear is more pliable and will maintain the results after heat therapy. By contrast, fake, plastic ones tend to go back to their original shape and condition once the heat is turned off. In that case, there's no lasting change, only a false, temporary alteration.

III Put Them On Ice

If turning up the heat isn't your thing, then there's always the cold treatment. Unlike the hands on effort required to stretch a shoe in the previous methods (or "feet on" effort to be exact), the cold approach takes much less activity on your part.

Take two baggies and fill them quarter full with water. Zip the bags up correctly, as it's crucial to keep everything bottled up and sealed. Slide the baggies into the offensive footwear and place them in the freezer.

Once in the freezer, you can forget about them for a while. Out of sight, out of mind. When you finally remember to pull them out, (thank goodness for Christmas turkeys or they may have been in there indefinitely) let the shoes thaw until the soles release the bags that have been held captive. Typically, a shoe will stretch a half or full size using this technique.

Unfortunately, the fit doesn't usually conform to the desired shape of your foot because the shoe will stretch in the direction of least resistance. The softer the material, the more wonky the results. Be warned though, some styles don't respond well to the cold and their finish may be irreversibly damaged from freezer burn.

Even if a pair of shoes has stretched and looks okay from the outside, people often find they are no longer wearable, due to the awkward shape. What a shame to damage soles so.

IV Shoe Stretchers

If you're willing to shell out a modest amount, you can buy a shoe stretching device that will slowly work out the fabric or leather over time. By turning knobs, the length and width of the shoe can be pushed and prodded with moderate results. It's not precise, and it does take a bit of time and money, but some people like this method.

V The Cobbler

For shoes we love, we would be much wiser to leave them in the skilled hands of the Cobbler. He examines each foot, and will gently work the shoe to fit over time. This is a more costly and time-consuming method, but the results are typically great, if not perfect!

Ladies, it's painful to be in unforgiving soles. And, it's not fun to be stretched either. Most of us try to fix our problems by ourselves, and as a result, end up in unnecessary pain, blasting those around us, or giving people the cold-shoulder. Other times, we spend money on self-help books in an effort to initiate behavior changes . . . but we don't get lasting transformation. The only permanent solution comes from a supernaturally changed soul.

Yes, far better to be placed in the hands of The Cobbler. Only He understands our design, is keenly aware of every unforgiving tight spot, and will shape us into what He has designed us to be.

Lack of forgiveness is one of the most damaging, problematic conditions we can have. Often the things that are holding us back are buried so deep in our souls we don't even know why we feel, speak and react the ways we do. We think it's "just who we are," or we blame our ethnicity, or think we're too old to change or beyond help. So we limp and stumble through life, believing the lie that we are destined to exist in a painful, broken, compromised state.

But the Cobbler hates to see us in disrepair. He is calling us to come and sit at His feet so that He can examine our souls— washing, repairing, and preparing us to do His work.

15

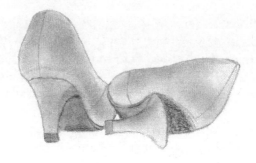

Broken Heels and Cracked Leather

*One small crack does not mean that you are
broken, it means that you were put to the test
and you didn't fall apart.*

~Linda Poindexter

Do you own a pair of shoes that you have had reconditioned
or repaired numerous times? I remember when I was a young
single gal, I once found the perfect pair of work pumps. They were
affordable, insanely cute, comfortable, and so versatile they could
go from office to evening. I bought pairs in white, blue, and red. I
loved these shoes, but the electric blue pair was especially stunning.

One day, while wearing these love-affair shoes, I felt one
foot buckle as I was crossing a busy intersection. Placing my weight
on my toes, I limped to the curb to inspect the damage. It was not
good. The two-inch tapered heel had snapped halfway down. The
leather was still perfect, but the core was broken. I hobbled

through the day, laughing at my predicament, while silently mourning the possible death of my favorite shoes.

Now, my mother had taught me to be frugal, so I wasn't about to just toss the pretties. Instead, when I got home, I pulled out my tiny toolbox and found a few finishing nails. I held the shoe and gently tapped a long, thin nail up through the rubber heel pad and into the broken chunk of wood. It seemed to mend the break, so I added one more nail for good measure. Pleased with my own resourcefulness, I placed the repaired pumps back amongst my shoes.

A few weeks later, I grabbed them and took a few test steps around my basement to be sure the heel held. Confident they were secure, I headed out the door to work. It was only as I walked on the sidewalk toward my car that I discovered one shoe made a distinctive clack, whereas the other clicked. With no time to go back and change shoes, I kept going. Besides, most of the office was carpeted.

Click, clack; click, clack.

I never realized how much bare floor the building actually had until I clicked and clacked around it that day. I'm sure my face was flushed every time I went vertical. The sound of my unique footsteps reminded me of Captain Hook.

In an attempt to quiet the "clack", I adjusted my step to try to avoid the nail heads and make more contact with the remaining rubber. As I did, the heel shifted under my foot. Cringing, I pulled the pump off, only to see the heel slightly askew and the tip of one nail protruding through the leather. While my quick fix had made the broken shoe somewhat functional, it was apparent that something was still not quite right.

I stored the broken heeled shoes with my others for a while, but I never wore them again. I was far too self-conscious and feared they would leave me stranded in their compromised state. Oh, but how pretty the toes still looked on my small shelf of shoes . . . useless . . . but pretty.

Perhaps a cobbler could have peeled back the leather to properly repair the heel, but I was young and had no idea such a profession existed. Eventually, these beauties got tossed into the garbage.

151

Years later, I discovered that improperly repaired heels are not the only things that snap.

Tired after a long day, I was working in the kitchen when I snapped and stomped all over my poor, unsuspecting husband, Don. No idea why. He stood there, mouth agape, eyebrows crushed together. I'm not too sure who was more shocked.

A few seconds passed before his face softened. He embraced me (a move that was equally brave and naïve on his part), but before I could react and pull away, he quietly whispered, "Old hurts; I'm sorry," and left me alone to process.

I rested my hands on the kitchen counter and bowed my head in embarrassment. *What was that? Where did that come from? What did he mean, "old hurts"?*

Moments passed before I realized that *this* irrational behavior was actually about *that*. "That" being something completely unrelated.

I had reacted to a minor infraction on his part—something that a "normal" person would have laughed off, but for me, brought on a tsunami of emotion, hurtful accusations, and tears. His teasing had hit a nerve and unleashed an arsenal of ugly that had little to do with what he said, and everything to do with a deeply buried pain from my past—an "old hurt". Clearly this was not a first assault. Hubby had seen a milder version of this broken reaction before.

Later, I apologized for my craziness. The more we talked it out, the more the ignored, festering hurt came into focus. What had been buried and hidden in the dark was now exposed to the light. I had managed for decades to adjust and shift my life in order to keep hobbling along, but my coping skills were clearly *clicking* and *clacking* all over other people's lives. It was time to get real and do whatever it took to properly fix my broken state.

When I read over the various survey comments, I saw areas of vulnerability that left many women to react off-kilter to "attacks" by others. For example, our Betty Boot was a bit of a people pleaser and had trouble saying "no". Over time she began to resent others. Stella Stiletto was frustrated with Betty needing her help too often, and with Penny Loafer for being such a . . . loafer. Meanwhile, our practical pump, Paisley—who's sturdy and sensible—saw all this toe stepping and slip sliding in the foyer, but couldn't seem to round everyone up and keep things in order.

Similar things happen far too often in our churches. As a result, there are blowups. Words are hurled—not gently specifically directed to fix real issues—but haphazardly, with dirt ending up everywhere over false and absolutely silly stuff. Like choosing the color of the nursery.

Yes, it seems the kicks and rips we take and inflict are not always about "this" but actually about "that".

We become exhausted and fed up. We interpret everything through the lens of our past, and too often we do not see things for what they truly are.

That day, when I wounded my sweet man, I was finally ready to find real healing.

It wasn't fun to face my painful layers. However, as I did, it became clear that I needed to take some time to slowly and thoroughly peel back the hurts and issues. This was not the time for a quick, cosmetic fix.

There are times when we need to pull ourselves away from our closeted lives and spend some concentrated time with the Cobbler. I speak to so many hurting women who have exhausted themselves trying to do "self-help" temporary fixes on things that need The Cobbler's hands. For me, He worked through the hearts, hands, and ears of Spirit-filled friends who specialize in helping people break free from past hurts and bondages. My prayer is that each of you who struggle with this will find a safe someone who will walk you through the following steps:

Step 1 – Talk! Write! Pray!

The first thing I had to do was talk. The Bible says that we are to "confess our sins one to another". A lot of the damage to my soul was not self-inflicted but arose from sexual abuse and several sexual assaults. Through this, *sin was inflicted on me*. Telling others about it was huge for me, and the fact I could do so with two people who loved me—never judging—was critical to my healing.

Many women have spoken to me about sexual abuse and assaults. Several of them told me it was the first time they had ever spoke of it. Most of those who held their secrets were my age or older. This comes as no surprise.

My abuse came to light in the 1970s, and the way sexual abuse was handled in the church was by confrontation, prayer, repentance (sometimes) by the offender, and then the classic, "Now, God has forgiven and forgotten, so we must too. Never speak to anyone about this."

Or at least, that is how it unfolded in my case. I was to keep quiet, and I did.

Years later, when I was sexually assaulted again at a youth event, my childhood programming stuck. I never told. Anyone. Not even my best female friend of over thirty years. I trusted no one, and fear tethered me, affecting my health.

From childhood, the hand of the abusive man who covered my mouth kept me gagged and stifled for years. But all that changed when as an adult, I finally spoke the truth out loud to my friends. In that moment, his imaginary hand was released and his phantom control broken. I could finally cry and share, and as I did, the boogie man grew smaller and smaller. Immediately, the enemy's power over me was weakened. My friends encouraged me to soul search and write down a list of the enemy's favorite labels, lies, tools, and strongholds from my past. Some of these confessions were my own sins; others were patterns of generational weaknesses (things like divorce, addiction, occult practices, astrology, fortune telling, and adultery). For the first time, I could see patterns emerging. Like an Achilles heel, Satan placed weaknesses in our family that plagued me, and most of my siblings and cousins.

Having written them down, we talked about each one. Some were just a quick "confession", while others were dealt with a bit deeper.

Then, using the list, we prayed. I confessed and released any and all the things that had held me captive. Some were just ink on the page, and I felt nothing as I prayed and let those issues go. Others were deep-rooted. I cried, pulling off the discount labels the enemy had placed on my soul. In joyful defiance, and with newfound understanding and authority, I tore down the walls the enemy had placed in and around my heart.

The hardest part of this peeling back process was being willing to stretch and offer forgiveness. This was somewhat painful, and I am told I not alone in this struggle. As tough as it is to forgive those who have wounded us, we also need to forgive ourselves for some things. I was privileged to walk through this process with one precious friend who prayed fairly stoically through many layers, but when it was time to forgive herself for something, she broke hard. Sweet tears of release were a blessing to see as I held her and wept alongside. Sometimes the labels we put on ourselves can be the most stubborn to release.

Then there's the big one. We seldom discuss or want to address this last layer, but many times we harbor unforgiveness towards The Cobbler. We question Him or are angry that He designed us the way He did. We wonder why He has allowed so many scuffs and so much brokenness in our lives. Often, this is the core of our soul damage. It was for me.

Having not seen any earthly justice for my assaults, I questioned and was angry with God for years until one day I found major comfort in 2 Samuel 22. I still refer to it often, to gain comfort when the enemy tries to trip me. Here is an excerpt:

"In my distress I called upon the Lord; to my God I called.
From his temple he heard my voice, and my cry came to his ears.
"Then the earth reeled and rocked; the foundations of the heavens trembled and quaked, because he was angry.

Smoke went up from his nostrils, and devouring fire from his mouth; glowing coals flamed forth from him. He bowed the heavens and came down; thick darkness was under his feet.
He rode on a cherub and flew; he was seen on the wings of the wind.
He made darkness around him his canopy, thick clouds, a gathering of water.

Out of the brightness before him coals of fire flamed forth.
The Lord thundered from heaven, and the Most High uttered his voice.
And he sent out arrows and scattered them; lightning, and routed them.
Then the channels of the sea were seen; the foundations of the world were laid bare, at the rebuke of the Lord, at the blast of the breath of his nostrils.

"He sent from on high, he took me; he drew me out of many waters.
He rescued me from my strong enemy, from those who hated me,

155

for they were too mighty for me.
They confronted me in the day of my calamity, but the LORD was my
support.

He brought me out into a broad place; he rescued me because he
delighted in me."

(2 Samuel 22:7-20)

Every time I read this Scripture, I imagine this is my Savior's reaction when He witnesses any injustice. We women adore a great love story with dragons and damsels . . . but what a romantic twist in God's version. He is fierce as He swoops down to rescue us, smoke coming from His nostrils, wiping out our adversaries. Can you feel His anger? His love? His protection?

We don't actually get to witness this in our earthly realm, but this is Truth. This is the heavenlies. He sees. He has rescued us, and given us ways to survive the enemy's hits, whatever he may throw at us. Knowing this, I can't help but believe The Cobbler has a unique purpose for each of us and our stories.

Yes, there have been times when I have asked the Lord, "Why?" Why didn't God swoop in and *stop* the abuse I went through for twelve years as a child? Why did He allow so many other men to assault me in my teen and adult years?

I've come to accept that answers are not always found on this side of heaven. However, I know that my God, El Roi—The God Who Sees—is in control, and His vengeance is sweet. What the devil tried to do to destroy me, Jesus undid at the cross. He set me free and has used my testimony to help other women break free from their pasts. To God be the glory. What's happened cannot be undone, but we have the choice to stay bitter and broken, or to get repaired and be used.

We need to find peace in our stories. To no longer ask Him, "Why?" Instead, to sit humbly at the feet of The Cobbler and quietly whisper, "Why not? Use me as You see fit. May my life be a living sacrifice."

Don't do what I did for all those years when I limped along and used my brokenness as an excuse to hide in my closet. Let Him restore your life. Jump into His story. Ask Him to cleanse, heal and equip you to go into battle and make the enemy pay for what he's done to you. We are in a war, and it's time to take on the enemy.

Again, the first thing we need to do upon sitting with The Cobbler, ladies, is to talk. And to bring someone along with us. It's a scary thing to sometimes share with others, but finding a safe place to offload is key. This is where so many of our scuffs and brokenness are exposed, laid bare for His examination and repair. Because until we get the healing we need, we can't be properly used for the amazing, fantastic purposes He's designed us to do.

Step 2 – Give it up

At the end of a busy workday, the floor of a Cobbler's shop is covered in dirt, dried glue, broken shoelaces, and rusty grommets. On his workbench, beautifully restored footwear waits to be claimed and utilized again. The Cobbler sweeps up the discarded shards and carefully dumps the junk back into the soles from whence it came.

Is that right? No, of course not! That would be ludicrous, but that is what our enemy would love us to do—to keep picking up and dragging around the things The Cobbler has removed from our lives. Satan loves it when we wallow in our past and flog ourselves.

No, having identified and laid the lies down at the foot of the cross, they are no longer our label or weakness. We have to disassociate ourselves from those things already cleansed from our lives.

Take the discarded labels and give them up.

Yet, it appears many of us like to hold on to our catalog of junk.

I teach a weekend retreat where we begin on Friday night by giving each woman a stone. By the end of the night, we encourage them to take that rock and write on it a label or lie that is holding them captive. Words like: ugly, stupid, unloved, useless, whore, addict . . . On Saturday, after a time of coming to grips with the truth of who they are in Christ, they go with a sister to a nearby body of water, pray, claim their freedom in agreement, and fling the rock into the pond, river, lake, or ocean. (Micah 7:19)

Yet, at every retreat, there is someone who has a hard-time releasing their rock.

Often, we become too entwined with our false identities. To let go would mean losing the only sense of self we have, no matter how distorted. It would require us to stop living a life of excuses and actually rise up out of our pits to do something bigger than ourselves. Ouch. It's so much easier to tuck that hard stone back into our pocket or purse and lug it around . . . or keep it in our shoe and limp painfully through life. To be restored by The Cobbler and set free might just mean that we have to step out of the goodwill box and be available to be used for His honor and glory.

Once again, fear or beliefs that we are unworthy or incapable hold us captive.

It breaks my heart to see any woman in bondage. It truly does. I recall meeting with one young gal and her mother privately in my room. The daughter had been "dragged" to the retreat by her well-meaning mother, and her wounds were deep, with layer upon layer of hurt. She talked and I listened.

I've heard it all over the years, but this young girl had multiple "unforgiveable" harms. With her mother interrupting several times, I knew that an hour was only going to scratch at the first layer. The two women needed to meet often at the cross— separately and together—to break the cycle of abuse and enabling behaviors. Although heartbreaking to hear her story, it was also a blessing as I saw the chains start to loosen.

Yes, I've seen some women restored supernaturally and instantly from their "stuff". Hallelujah! Others need repeat and sometimes supervised appointments at the foot of the cross for complete restoration. Sometimes The Cobbler meets and works One-on-one. Other times He may use a friend, and on occasion, spirit filled, gifted women and men. It's much like how Jesus didn't always physically heal blind people the same way.

Sometimes He spoke it:
And Jesus said to him, 'Recover your sight; your faith has made you well.'

(Luke 18:42)

Sometimes He touched them:

Then he touched their eyes, saying, 'According to your faith be it done to you.'

(Matthew 9:29)

And sometimes He made mud and engaged them in the healing process:

Having said these things, he spit on the ground and made mud with the saliva. Then he anointed the man's eyes with the mud and said to him, 'Go, wash in the pool of Siloam' (which means Sent). So he went and washed and came back seeing.

(John 9:6-7)

We need to be soft and yielding in the Cobbler's hands. He knows what needs to be done; it's our job to be pliable and open to receive his healing and restoration, in whatever way he chooses. We also need to be careful not to point fingers of judgment toward others who are receiving the Master Cobbler's touch in a different way.

Let Him swoop into your soul today and rescue you. If your Christian walk is boring, you're doing it wrong. Join us and walk strong and with confidence in the restored shoe The Cobbler has designed and called you to be.

16

Buff and Polish

Give a girl the right shoes, and she can conquer the world!

~Marilyn Monroe

Once we've been cleaned up and repaired, we need to be mindful of where we walk.

I remember one Easter, my mother sent my brothers, myself and our respective girlfriends/boyfriend on a scavenger hunt. The clues led us into all sorts of situations and friends' yards. Being that we were all in our twenties, this was a bit awkward . . . but secretly fun! The young man I was dating was extremely caught up in preventing his expensive, freshly polished shoes from getting dirty. He tip-toed through the muddy grass patches, wincing with each spot that landed on the bright polished, multi-colored shoes (it was the eighties and Miami Vice fashion was all the rage). He had worn these pricey loafers for the Easter worship service—not to be traipsing through an obstacle course. These shoes were for showin', not for scavengin'! After all, precious, pricey soles should not be dragged through the mud.

When we see ourselves as The Cobbler sees us, and recognize the value that we hold in His eyes, we too should be careful of not falling back into the mire. No longer should we consider ourselves as disposable booties (like the ones surgeons wear over their shoes in the operating room) but rather as priceless treasures, made clean and designed for His work and purpose.

Still, there will be times when we may not really be thrilled with the style of shoe we have been called to be. I struggled in my Cindy Solo season, and I've heard testimonies from others about painful bunions and blisters from walking as "misfits" in church foyers. This doesn't mean we can go hide in the back of our closets.

Wherever we are at this moment, whatever stage of repair we're in, we need to remain functional as The Cobbler is working things out in our lives. We need to accept our situation and seek to be used, just as we are.

Buffing and polishing takes work from the Cobbler and is sometimes painful to receive, but with each pass of His hand, hard, abrasive bristles cause His shoes to shine. Even a tough boot benefits from a good brushing. It's a key step to make us a *true* light in this dark world.

There have been seasons of my life when I pouted and hid due to the condition of my soul. I would arrive late to church and leave early, determined to not let anyone see the true state of my life. If accosted in the foyer, I would smile and lie through my teeth. What a wasteful, selfish season.

There is an alternative way. We can be victorious and honest at the same time.

We need to praise Him through the pain.

When my husband, Don, was recovering from open-heart surgery, even though his ticker was deemed better-than-ever, he was still suffering and in a fair amount of discomfort. He didn't wake, jump up, and resume his life. He needed time to rest and recover . . . and the healing was painful.

Although Don is not a whiner, he wasn't exactly singing joyful choruses either. Yet, aware that the enemy doesn't sleep during our off days, he knew that God had him on this cardiac ward for a reason. And Don also knew the key to taking Satan down.

And they have conquered him by the blood of the Lamb and by the word of their testimony, for they loved not their lives even unto death.
(Revelation 12:11)

While hubby clenched his teeth and struggled in his recovery, with the Holy Spirit's prompting, he also reached out and prayed for those on his ward who were struggling, too. As Don experienced setbacks and pain, his testimony of how The Cobbler saved and transformed his life became all the more powerful.

People crave authenticity and tend to listen and respect those who can relate to what they are going through.

"I think we often feel that we need to cope, look like we're coping, and always be smiling. I love it in our church that someone can cry when they need to, and that women rally around (e.g. last Sunday when a woman shared that she couldn't share emotionally with her husband about their daughter's cancer, and women just RALLIED around her. Beautiful to see!)"
~52-year-old Australian Practical Pump

By being selfish, fake, and avoiding fellowship during my painful seasons, I not only slowed down my own healing, I also robbed my sisters-in-Christ from the blessings that come from authentic spiritual service. As The Cobbler buffs and polishes us, we shouldn't hide in the closet but allow others to come alongside. I know, I know, we've all probably been marred and have scuffs from gossip and fake fellowship. Discernment is needed before we expose some of our "stuff" as there are some whose motives are evil. Which is why establishing healthy relationships during our easier seasons is crucial so that we'll have support ready when we need it. Women who we can truly trust.

Left on our own, this is not our natural default, but by The Cobbler's power and amazing grace, having taken a stroll in the soles of our sisters, we can and will drop the spirit of deception and judgment. I pray we can take on the roles to which He has called us. It *is* possible to stop stepping on each other's toes and I

162

believe, with God's help, we can change our souls in many ways. I pray that:

- we will be able to cry, laugh, and pray together without fear;
- we will throw mud at the enemy, instead of at each other;
- the dirt our enemy tosses our way will not stick, but will slide off our polished, sealed soles.

Now that we've spent some time with The Cobbler, hopefully we've come to accept our own shapes, sizes, seasons, and functions for His honor and glory. We've also taken a quick stroll inside the soles of our sisters, so now, filled with compassion, we'll stop before we stomp. We'll consider that perhaps there maybe something going on in their lives that we don't know. Amazing Grace. It's all about grace. For ourselves and for others.

With that change of heart and by functioning in the Spirit, perhaps Running shoes will see our love and will run back through our church doors (however big or small those doors may be).

17

Proper Care and Storage

If I ever let my head down . . . it will be just to admire my shoes!

I have a friend who is a shoe fashionista. She takes footwear very seriously, even designating an entire closet to them. To her, a shoe is an investment, and it needs to be properly cared for and safely stored.

Which brings us now to the last lap on this journey we've taken together. How do we keep our soles from falling back into a religious, dead walk that leaves carnage along our paths?

It's important to examine our souls and soles often. I mean, have you ever taken your pooch for a walk around the block, only to smell something nasty as you walk back in the front door? You stop, turn over your sneaker, and there it is—yup. Just because you pick up after your dog doesn't mean your neighbors pick up after theirs. Can you imagine what it would be like if you didn't notice what was on the bottom of your sneaker, and you tossed them straight inside your front door coat closet? It wouldn't take long for the whole house to stink. If not dealt with, your home would be an unpleasant place to be, and few would want to visit.

The enemy loves to toss crud at us. Especially when he sees that we are now clean and restored. No, Satan does not like to see us healthy, happy and being used. He wants us to feel like misfits, with labels gumming up our soles.

But no! We've come too far to let him niggle his way back into our hearts and minds. So what do we do? How do we walk consistently in victory and not let his lies weigh us down?

We need to be solid in our understanding of who we are in Christ. Only then can we stroll securely in our identity and authority. Otherwise, we will stumble around like Paisley Pump—getting our freedom, but not keeping it. Walk with me now as I share something that may help.

A few years ago, my day job was as a training coordinator for law enforcement officers. During my first few weeks on the job, a few of the women officers invited me out for dinner after work. As they were off duty before me, we agreed that I would meet them at a local restaurant.

When I got to the restaurant, I couldn't see any of them. Confused, I thought for a moment that I had been stood up. Then, all of a sudden, a drop-dead gorgeous woman grabbed me by the arm. (Note: please don't ever do that to a Penny Loafer). I stared at her, and then burst out laughing. She was completely unrecognizable. At work, the female officers are required to keep their hair pulled up and off their faces. Most of them don't pack on the war paint, preferring to keep their look minimal and professional.

We walked to our table, and I marveled that even her walk was different. She was wearing heels and had a bit of a wiggle to her hips . . . nothing like the march she took in her steel-toed work boots. She was 100% feminine.

The next time we worked together, I watched this gal as she entered the building. She walked with serious authority—shoulders back, badge visible, commanding respect.

Which led me to consider the training these women had gone through to become peace officers, and how they transform themselves when they don their uniforms.

165

First, they have to complete months of grueling physical and mental training. They are drilled and tested until they can prove that they "get it". Upon graduation, they are issued a shiny badge that they wear with pride. It shows they have authority to enforce the criminal code.

Ah, the code book. It's a rather hefty volume. About the same size actually as another Good Book you may know. The officers have to study the criminal code and be able to know where to find the proper statutes and rules to apply. Of course, they don't memorize the whole thing—but it's their guidebook and is crucial to assist them in knowing exactly what is and is not enforceable. When they graduate, it is a proud moment of accomplishment.

Let's take a walk in the boots of a newly graduated officer:

Having successfully finished her course, she is now on her first shift. With her hair pulled up, she clips on her badge and walks as one with authority.

Suddenly, her training is put to the test. She recognizes that a law is being broken and she needs to take the rule breaker captive.

Removing the handcuffs from her duty belt pouch, the officer opens up the first cuff and snaps it around the culprit's wrist. Then she takes the cuffed arm around the person's back and secures his second hand. This renders him less of a threat so he can be put in cells until passed on to the court. As she does this, she quotes the charge against him, referring to the code book.

What on earth does this have to do with us?

Everything.

1. We too take on a new identity when we are born again. We have a badge that identifies us as being the **B**lood-bought children of the Most High God.

2. As daughters of the King, we have been given **A**uthority, and with that comes the responsibility to study His Word so we will know how we are to walk.

3. We also have **H**andcuffs, and we use them to take captive any thoughts that would be contrary to what we know is true.

I think we often get the first two points nailed down, but we mess up with the third.

How ridiculous would it be if you were to watch this new officer handcuff the "bad guy", but instead of leading him to the judge, the officer left the culprit handcuffed to the back of her duty belt? After all, it was her arrest; shouldn't she be responsible to keep him under control?

Of course not! That would be crazy. The officer would not be effective, nor would she be able to walk safely for the rest of her shift.

No, the officer knows she needs to hand the lawbreaker over to the judge.

Ladies, like I said, this is where so many of us mess up. We are not handing over our "bad guys" to Jesus.

We have been washed and the labels removed, but the enemy keeps trying to stick those lies back on us. Thoughts tumble in our head like a relentless dryer, spinning round and round. Satan lied to Eve and he's still lying today:

He was a murderer from the beginning, and does not stand in the truth, because there is no truth in him. When he lies, he speaks out of his own character, for he is a liar and the father of lies.

(John 8:44b)

We wrestle with his lies all day as they continue to hang on our backs. No matter how much we study the Word, or remind ourselves of our new identity in Christ, we are often weighed-down, struggling with these rebels from our past. All the lies and obstacles that dull the truth and light He wants us to walk in.

"For though we walk in the flesh, we are not waging war according to the flesh. For the weapons of our warfare are not of the flesh but have divine power to destroy strongholds. We destroy arguments and every lofty opinion raised against the knowledge of God, and take every thought captive to obey Christ, being ready to punish every disobedience, when your obedience is complete."

(2 Corinthians 10:3-6 ESV)

Keeping that ridiculous visual of the officer running around with her enemy strapped to her back, here's a quick trick to help nail down this freedom-keeping-truth into our souls:

Sheep say BAH

Each time we go to The Cobbler, we leave clean, walking with confidence in the shoes He has created us to be. We walk happily down the road in our beautifully restored shoes, when suddenly the enemy sticks out his foot and tries to trip us. That's when we need to dig those darling heels in and apply the BAH truth.

Say it with me . . . sheep say **BAH**! (Jesus calls us His sheep.)

1. We are a **B**LOOD-bought child of the Most High God (Acts 20:28)
2. All **A**UTHORITY has been given to us (Luke 10:19). Throw scripture!
3. **H**ANDCUFF (take captive) those thoughts that try to put us back into a broken, dirty state, and then pass the lie to Jesus (2 Corinthians 10:5).

I sometimes actually speak these three steps out loud, especially when the condemning thoughts are relentless. For instance, if the enemy is prodding me with one of my many fear triggers, I paraphrase: "I am a blood-bought child of the living God and 'He has given me a spirit not of fear but of power and love and self-control'. (2 Timothy 1:7) I handcuff this silly lie of fear, and I give it to you, Lord Jesus!"

Now that might seem like a mouthful, but it has become second nature to me. If you haven't memorized scripture, I encourage you to start. We need to stand on the Word, yes . . . but flinging it at the enemy is pretty effective, too. So equip yourself. (You can write out some notecards with strengthening verses personalized to you—it won't take long until they're memorized).

Jesus, when He was being tempted in the wilderness threw scripture to combat the devil; three times He said, 'It is written'. Of course, the enemy used scripture too. Why? Because even he knows there is power in it.

My beautiful friend was constantly bombarded with accusing thoughts from her past. She couldn't get relief even when she was sleeping as her dreams were tormenting her too. When she learned the BAH truth, a few days later she was smiling from ear to ear. She was free! The first few days she had to "handcuff" often, but gradually the enemy gave up. He hates hearing the Word of God!

Here are some great "handcuffing" verses to keep tucked in your souls:

"Be strong and courageous. Do not fear or be in dread of them, for it is the Lord your God who goes with you. He will not leave you or forsake you."

(Deuteronomy 31:6)

"Casting all your anxieties on him, because he cares for you."

(1 Peter 5:7)

"Even though I walk through the valley of the shadow of death, I will fear no evil, for you are with me; your rod and your staff, they comfort me."

(Psalm 23:4)

"Fear not, for I am with you; be not dismayed, for I am your God; I will strengthen you, I will help you, I will uphold you with my righteous right hand."

(Isaiah 41:10)

"Do not be anxious about anything, but in everything by prayer and supplication with thanksgiving let your requests be made known to God. And the peace of God, which surpasses all understanding, will guard your hearts and your minds in Christ Jesus."

(Philippians 4:6-7)

"He gives power to the faint, and to him who has no might he increases strength."

(Isaiah 40:29)

This is powerful stuff, girls! I struggled for years to stay free, and I still use BAH regularly. The simple exercise has changed my walk and my life. I encourage you to find a sister-shoe and learn this together. We need to get freedom . . . and keep it!

I am weeping as I write, praying that if you're wrestling with the accuser, you will embrace this and walk in the freedom of **BAH**.

To Box or to Hang?

So now that we are keeping our soles clean, and we know how to protect ourselves from getting stuck again with the lies from our past . . . what next?

Should your soles be in a box . . . or left out to hang? Where are you to go to learn, grow and fellowship?

Wherever you end up, before settling your soles, make sure that the leaders of that fellowship are Bible believing, born again, spirit filled teachers of the Word. If the Bible is not read or quoted at any time during the meeting, I suggest you leave. I'm saying this not to be judgmental, but because as a teacher sent by God, it's my responsibility to help keep your souls safe.

His Word is . . . His Word. We need it . . . every time and everywhere we have church.

Be sure they lift high the name of Jesus—the True Jesus from the Bible—and give reverence before the Throne of God.

Your fellowship should be one that is not merely a namby-pamby, feel-good, positive thinking, cheerleading rah-rah squad. Weekly messages that are only a peppy, encouraging talk are dangerous, sending souls into the world ill-prepared and unaware of spiritual battles. Those kinds of lessons can result in many false conversions—people who think they are saved because they go to church each week, but are not. My husband regularly attended two different churches for several years and did not know Christ but thought he did. Jesus said:

> *Not everyone who says to me, 'Lord, Lord,' will enter the kingdom of heaven, but the one who does the will of my Father who is in heaven. On that day many will say to me, 'Lord, Lord, did we not prophesy in your name, and cast out demons in your name, and do many mighty works in your name?' And then will I declare to them, 'I never knew you; depart from me, you workers of lawlessness.'* (Matthew 7:21-23)

Which is why today when I turn on certain "Christian" talk shows, I am sometimes dismayed to see "leaders" who should be using their massive platforms to make people aware of their fallen state and need of a Savior serve candy-coated messages instead. They are focusing on what makes people feel good—telling people they can lead better, more prosperous lives.

Eternity, Christ, and other people are to be our focus, not making our own earthly lives comfy. I fear we have been fed the lie that our lives are "good enough" and that The Cobbler doesn't expect anything from us. This is not what I've read in The Word.

So be sure that your church teaches repentance. That there is a judgement coming for all, and that Jesus' cleansing blood is the only answer. That living for Christ does not mean a life without struggles, pain or sacrifice. Walking as a disciple of Christ is not a guaranteed easy way . . . but it's the only way.

"The people weren't why I left the church. Yes they can be cliquey, but really, who cares? I left because I realized one day I couldn't deal with the exclusive beliefs of the Christian church anymore. No one has a corner on truth, but the attitude is they know it all and everyone else is going to hell. I guess I'm more of a United Church person now, but why bother?"

~52-year-old Canadian

Recently, a great friend asked me how I knew that Jesus is the only way. She believes He was a good man—a prophet even— but that all roads lead to heaven. God is too good that any should perish.

Immediately I recalled a lesson from C. S. Lewis. I believe the Holy Spirit brought it to mind just when I needed it.

I asked her, "Do you have any doubt that Christ lived, walked, and died on this earth?"

"No, he is a documented historical figure."

We discussed how the whole world's calendars are structured to refer to his life and death—no matter what religion.

"So we do agree that He was either the Son of God—the Christ—or a good man and a prophet?"

With a big smile, she nodded in agreement.

"Well then, here's the thing. Jesus said, *'I am the way, the truth and the life. No one comes to the Father except through me'*. (John 4:6) So He is either who He said He was—The Only Way and the Son of God—or He was a lunatic or a liar . . . and a lunatic or a liar cannot be considered a good man or a prophet.

"Along that same thought, if it's not in dispute that Jesus came as the Son of God, then why would a loving Father allow His only Son to go through such a painful death to pay for our sins if we could just be good or do good instead?"

I did not challenge or put down her religion or beliefs. (I've learned not to stomp on people's toes, but to speak the truth in love and let The Cobbler do the rest). I smiled and left her with that to chew on. She knows where to find me, and knows that I love her unconditionally—no matter what road she chooses.

So I leave you with that question, too.

It's not that we Christians are arrogant and narrow minded to believe what we believe. We just know what we know. Those of us who walk with Him every day feel His power and presence to the depth of our souls. He is not just "one way" . . . He is The *Only* Way.

Some wondered why I included the above "off-shoe" topic in the conclusion of this footwear book. Others said that I was "Preaching to the choir". I confess, that's exactly what I am doing. Because the choir sometimes needs to hear this message.

In fact, years ago, two different churches agreed to share a building in order to stretch their small budgets. After a few months of this arrangement, they decided to do a joint service in order to get to know each other and fellowship. I don't know how they determined which pastor was to preach, but the pastor who taught had a habit of always presenting the gospel to allow people to accept Christ at the end of each of his sermons. So he did. Imagine his surprise and joy when the first person who raised his hand and came to the front to give his life to Christ was the senior pastor of the other fellowship group. He had missed the truth! As did most of his congregation.

You see, I am convinced that a huge part of the problem within our churches is that many people are confessing Christ but don't really know Him, and they are definitely not yielding to Him as Lord. There's a saying, "Going to church doesn't make you a Christian any more than sitting on a shoe rack makes you a shoe". Or something like that.

So many people believe that they are "Christians" because their parents were Christians, they were baptized as babies, or because of where they are found on Sunday mornings. But that is the only evidence in their lives. Their interaction with each other is anything but godly. They can be vicious and ugly. I know. I was one of them. I faked it for years. It's not like I have it all together and I'm perfect now. Because I'm not. Far from it. Just ask my family. But the desire of my heart, and what I'm working towards is to be more Christ-like every day. It's a journey that I am walking out with my Lord.

Which is why when asked today if I am a Christian, I will often respond with a smile and, 'No, I'm a follower of Jesus' or 'No, I'm a Jesus lover.' Or, 'Well, that depends how you define a Christian.' Because that opens discussion to help bridge the gap that exists today between what a true believer, follower, and disciple of Christ is versus the poor reputation of those who are *just* churchgoers. Churchgoers are dangerous people. I know I was. I labeled myself as a Christian but at the same time, was not Spirit filled and as a result lacked the fruit of the Spirit in my life. I was portraying a terrible witness to others. Nobody would ever have wanted what I had. No one.

If you've walked with me thus far, I hope that you know my heart. There's a chance that some of you may be just where I was a few years ago.

It's not about the size, shape or style of your sole. It's about the eternal condition of your soul. Are you truly, born again? Are you daily in the Word of God, studying, applying and obeying His commands? Are you plugged into a Bible teaching group that teaches repentance, outreach and discipleship? Do you have a hunger to spend time with Jesus in one way or another? Are you walking in the joy of the Lord?

If your answer was "yes" to the questions above, is it your natural desire to do these things, or just a heavy obligation? Jesus *asks* his disciples to follow Him. When we are born-again, when we choose to walk with Him, it should be a love relationship; like a courtship where the two cannot stand to be apart for too long. This is what it's all about.

This is the key to not stepping on each other and for developing effective, loving relationships within and outside our church walls. Unbelievers will know we are Christians by our love . . . *because truly transformed, Spirit controlled people live differently. They love as He loves.*

Like Ruth Graham said, we are works in progress. Walking with The Lord does not mean that each step we take will be perfect. We'll still stumble around and mess up now and then— our lives will not be void of mistakes. But ladies, when we yield to Him daily, He will empower us and lead us to wonderful places we could have never imagined.

My prayer is that each of you, having taken a walk in your sisters' shoes, will remember to apply grace to your own souls and to others. Step out in faith and make your journey an exciting walk with The Cobbler . . . no matter what shoes you may find yourself in.

Now to Him who is able to keep you from stumbling, and to make you stand in the presence of His glory blameless with great joy, to the only God our Savior, through Jesus Christ our Lord, be glory, majesty, dominion and authority, before all time and now and forever. Amen.
(Jude 1:24-25 NASB)

Appendix A
Jesus Knows Your Name

The Bible tells of a man climbing a tree in order to get a clear view of Jesus. As Jesus passed by, He stopped, looked up into the branches and called out, "Zacchaeus, come down; I am coming to your house!" The really amazing thing is this—Jesus not only knew Zacchaeus was there, but Jesus knew his name!

Maybe it has never crossed your mind, but Jesus Knows Your Name!

Actually, He knows everything about you. He knows your successes and your failures; He knows your hopes and dreams; He knows your sorrow and fears. But here's something that's even more amazing—He loves you so much that He died for you! The Bible states that God showed His great love for us by sending Christ to die for us while we were still sinners.

Back to the man in the tree—obviously shaken and surprised, Zacchaeus scrambled down and welcomed Jesus into his house. The rest of the story describes the life changing impact that visit had upon him. This could be your story—today! The only requirements are that, like Zacchaeus, you move from being a cautious spectator and welcome Jesus into your life.

If you sense God calling your name, and you want Jesus in your life, consider finding a quiet place and then pray this prayer: "Lord Jesus Christ, I sense you are calling my name—and right now, I invite You into my life. Thank you for dying on the cross for me. Please forgive my sin, cleanse my heart, and fill me with the Holy Spirit. I thank you in the name of Jesus. Amen."

These three steps will help set the course of your new life:

1. Tell someone that today you became a Christian
2. Read the Bible. Begin with Luke's gospel, then the book of Acts—both in the New Testament.
3. Plug into a Bible teaching group or church.

Bible references referred to in this article: Luke 19:1-10; Jeremiah 31:3; Romans 5:8; 2 Peter 1:3

F.T. (A print-ready file for this brochure is downloadable for free at www.SolesDefiningSouls.com)

A Personal Note

Thank you so much for reading Soles Defining Souls. If you enjoyed it, please take a moment to leave a review at your favorite online retailer such as Amazon USA or Amazon CA.

I would also love to hear from you. Please join our community on Facebook (www.facebook.com/SolesDefiningSouls) or send me a quick email at Lori@LovingKindnessMinistries.ca.

Thanks again for spending some time with me and I hope and pray that your time was well spent. May you keep running close behind The Cobbler.

Blessings,

Lori

Book Two – Bag Ladies

My husband knows that if he loses me in a department store I can most likely be found in the purse and luggage area. It's my favorite place to peruse, which just about makes him crazy. He can't understand how I could possibly need another handbag . . . ever!

But it's not my fault—really it's not. The bags are lined up, some standing at attention, others hanging—all just waiting for my inspection. Who am I to keep them waiting? Typically, the bags are organized by their color, shape, or size, which makes the whole area esthetically pleasing and inviting.

This is not my bedroom; this place is in order.

You know what I'm talking about, ladies. Purses are our friends. Unlike other things in our closet that are known to give us grief when we retain a bit of water or carry a few extra pounds, bags are completely oblivious.

So why do we have all the bags we carry?

For all of our *stuff*, of course!

But, there comes a time when every woman needs to deal with her baggage . . . and oh, do we ever have a lot of things to clean out:

- Lunch bags—full of our emotions
- Shopping bags—expensive, retail therapy
- Backpacks—everyone else's junk
- and a closet full of other totes!

When it comes time for a clean out, we never quite know what we'll find, but to be sure, those sturdy satchels we cart around need to be purged.

Join me won't you, as we bravely examine the crud and the artifacts *Bag Ladies* hoard. Together we'll unpack some of the heavy stuff we needlessly carry!

Resources

Books Mentioned in Soles Defining Souls

Crazy Love, Francis Chan, David C Cook Publishing Company
Revised edition (4 Jan. 2013)
ISBN-13: 978-1434705945

5 Minutes with Jesus, Sheila Walsh, Thomas Nelson
(10 Sept. 2015)
ISBN-13: 978-0718032531

First 5 App, Proverbs 31 Ministries
Download at http://first5.org/

Lori's Favorite Bible Studies

Breaking Free, Beth Moore, LifeWay Christian Resources
5th Updated edition (1 Oct. 2009)
ISBN-13: 978-1415868027
(video lessons available at www.Lifeway.com)

Lord I want to Know You, Kay Arthur, WaterBrook Press
(21 Nov. 2000)
ISBN-13: 978-1578564392
(video lessons available at www.preceptministries.com)

Made in the USA
San Bernardino, CA
27 December 2018